TEACHING
ENGLISH LANGUAGE
LEARNERS

ACROSS THE
CONTENT AREAS

TEACHING
ENGLISH LANGUAGE
LEARNERS

ACROSS THE
CONTENT AREAS

JUDIE HAYNES and DEBBIE ZACARIAN

Alexandria, Virginia USA

1703 N. Beauregard St. • Alexandria, VA 22311-1714 USA
Phone: 800-933-2723 or 703-578-9600 • Fax: 703-575-5400
Web site: www.ascd.org • E-mail: member@ascd.org
Author guidelines: www.ascd.org/write

Gene R. Carter, *Executive Director;* Nancy Modrak, *Publisher;* Scott Willis, *Director, Book Acquisitions & Development;* Carolyn Pool, *Acquisitions Editor;* Julie Houtz, *Director, Book Editing & Production;* Ernesto Yermoli, *Editor;* Reece Quiñones, *Senior Graphic Designer;* Mike Kalyan, *Production Manager;* BMWW, *Typesetter;* Sarah Plumb, *Production Specialist*

All Web links in this book are correct as of the publication date below but may have become inactive or otherwise modified since that time. If you notice a deactivated or changed link, please e-mail books@ascd.org with the words "Link Update" in the subject line. In your message, please specify the Web link, the book title, and the page number on which the link appears.

PAPERBACK ISBN: 978-1-4166-0912-4   ASCD product #109032   n2/10
Also available as an e-book (see Books in Print for the ISBNs).

Quantity discounts for the paperback edition only: 10–49 copies, 10%; 50+ copies, 15%; for 1,000 or more copies, call 800-933-2723, ext. 5634, or 703-575-5634. For desk copies: member@ascd.org.

Library of Congress Cataloging-in-Publication Data

Haynes, Judie.
    Teaching English language learners across the content areas / Judie Haynes and Debbie Zacarian.
        p. cm.
    Includes bibliographical references and index.
    ISBN 978-1-4166-0912-4 (pbk. : alk. paper)   1. English language—Study and teaching (Elementary)—Foreign speakers.   2. English language—Study and teaching (Secondary)—Foreign speakers.   3. Second language acquisition.   I. Zacarian, Debbie.   II. Title.
    PE1128.A2H3836 2010
    428.2'4—dc22
                                                                            2009040131

20 19 18 17 16 15 14 13 12 11 10 09   1 2 3 4 5 6 7 8 9 10 11 12

TEACHING
ENGLISH LANGUAGE
LEARNERS | ACROSS THE CONTENT AREAS

FOREWORD

By Elizabeth Claire

The worst day in my life was my first day of school in the United States. I felt like an alien. . . . I didn't understand anything. I didn't know anybody at all. I was late to all of my classes. It was like a nightmare. I just sat down and put my head down on my desk. I wished for the end of the day, so I could go home.—C.M., a 7th grade ELL student

Stories like the one above are multiplied a thousand times each day across the United States as newcomers sit in mainstream classes at the mercy of their teacher's patience, sensitivity, and preparation for their arrival. Whether these newcomers spend the day bored and frustrated or engaged in meaningful activities and socializing with their classmates is all up to the subject area teacher for the greater part of their day. Newcomers form an increasingly large percentage of our public school population. They are tomorrow's workforce, citizens, and parents. What happens to them matters deeply to all of us.

When I was a mainstream teacher, before I became an ESL teacher, I certainly had plenty of sensitivity, but not much preparation, and my hands were more than full, so I know what the problems are from both sides of the table. I was often guilt-ridden because I didn't know how to find time to give the amount of attention these newcomers needed and still cover what had to be covered for English-fluent students.

Multiply me by 6.2 million teachers across the United States, most of whom teach classes that include English language learners.

Judie Haynes and Debbie Zacarian to the rescue.

It would be hard to imagine two more qualified educators to help mainstream teachers not only to assist ELLs so that they participate fully in class, but also to enhance the learning of the rest of the students at the same time.

I met Judie Haynes as she was giving a workshop for ESL teachers at New Jersey TESOL. We discovered that, by amazing coincidence, we had both considered writing a resource book for mainstream teachers of ELLs. We both were anguished by the plight of ELLs whose days in mainstream classes were filled with wasted time, embarrassment, and social isolation. We could see that these students would be marked for life by their experiences during their English-learning years. Society would pay for the absence of attention to their needs. Hoping to provide what was missing in the field, together we wrote *Classroom Teacher's ESL Survival Kits 1 and 2* (Prentice Hall, 1995 & 1996). Now, along with Debbie Zacarian, she has written a book that provides practical strategies for school principals, curriculum directors, supervisors, and, of course, mainstream teachers.

Judie taught for 29 years and has tirelessly trained the mainstream teachers both at her school and in other school districts around the United States. She wrote a column on elementary ESL issues for TESOL's *Essential Teacher*. Her last book, *Getting Started with English Language Learners: A Guide for Educators* (ASCD, 2007), helps classroom teachers and school administrators learn best practices for incorporating ELLs in school. That book has become a "must-read" in the field.

Debbie was also a columnist for TESOL's *Essential Teacher*, writing on issues for secondary teachers. As director of the Center for English Language Education and founding director of the Center for Advancing Student Achievement at the Hampshire Educational Collaborative in Northampton, Massachusetts, she has extensive experience with training classroom teachers to work with English language learners.

Now together, Judie and Debbie have joined forces to write the perfect book for educators—not a how-to from the ivory tower, but a guide from down in the trenches, with example after example of experiments and successes by mainstream teachers and school leaders. This book offers dozens of insightful and simple ways to plan for ELLs participating in a unit, incorporating them in groups where they can hear authentic language and be responsible for a role in the group. I was delighted to see that language in the text is down to earth; he book reads like a collection of short stories that teachers can quickly relate to.

The strategies in this book don't require that you do anything *extra*, just differently. The techniques that work with ELLs will enhance your lessons such that every one of your English-fluent students will benefit greatly as well.

If you are a teacher or administrator who has been struggling to secure ways for ELLs to participate in general education classes and school activities, you can be relieved. Teachers and administrators cannot read this book without having their perceptions altered or altering the lives of their ELLs. The book reads quickly, and opens eyes. With hands-on and visual learning a great part of lesson presentation, reports, projects, and testing, *all* students benefit, and you gain for yourself that remarkable feeling, remembered for a lifetime, of having made your students' days meaningful and powerful.

Elizabeth Claire
Founder and editor
Easy English News

ACKNOWLEDGMENTS

Our book was written with the support of many people.

Several classroom teachers from River Edge Public School in New Jersey—including Joann Frechette, Julie Mahoney, Patricia Wondra, Susan Meldonian, Laura Menzella, Cathy Danahy, Monica Schnee, and Nancy Du Bois—generously shared their expertise.

We spent long hours collaborating on this manuscript and appreciate the support of our families—especially our husbands, Joe and Matt.

We thank ASCD acquisitions editor Carolyn Pool for guiding our efforts during the writing stage, and copy editor Ernesto Yermoli for helping us with the editing of the final manuscript. They both contributed greatly to this book.

The adage "many fingers make a hand" speaks to the gratitude that we wish to express.

INTRODUCTION

The audience for *Teaching English Language Learners Across the Content Areas* is teachers, supervisors, curriculum specialists, principals, and superintendents who are working with English language learners (ELLs) in their classrooms. This book is the result of our combined experience working with ELLs: Judie taught elementary and middle school ELLs for 28 years and has been working with teachers of ELLs for the last 16 years; Debbie worked with high school ELLs for six years, administered K–12 English language education for over 20 years, and taught at a university for over a decade where she designed and developed courses for general classroom, secondary subject-matter, special education, resource, and English as a Second Language (ESL) teachers, as well as for administrators who taught English to ELLs. Debbie directs a professional development, consulting, and support center for teachers and administrators of ELLs.

Educators are teaching a rapidly growing number of ELLs in U.S. schools, yet most public school teachers are not trained to do so. As a result, they are challenged to find effective ways to ensure that ELLs are actively participating in content area instruction. This is particularly so because many ELLs receive limited instruction in ESL.

We believe that students' success is highly correlated with their engagement in the learning process. Although statewide assessments are often used as measures of student success, we worry about the impact of tests that are given when students are not yet competent in English. Learning English is a developmental process that occurs over a period of years. It is dependent on the comprehensibility, quality, and sustainability of language and content learning experiences. Although advocating for fair testing is important, modifying instruction to make it accessible to ELLs is at the core of what must occur.

Through our own experience, we know that ELLs need to be instructed by teachers who create and deliver lessons that effectively teach both content and the English language while promoting active student engagement. It is our goal to help teachers build classroom and school environments where all students, including ELLs, can flourish. We want to show elementary grade-level, secondary subject-matter, special education, and resource teachers; curriculum directors; administrators; support staff; and other stakeholders how to involve their ELL students in content activities with the whole class to the greatest extent possible. To that end, this book will focus on how teachers can improve student academic language and literacy learning in language arts, math, science, and social studies classes.

The ideas and tools that we present in this book will help teachers strengthen students' capacity to learn content vocabulary and concepts, activate students' background knowledge, modify content area materials in ways that specifically address language and content learning, and communicate content information to ELLs. The book is organized around strategies for working with ELLs in a content area class. These strategies include

- Developing classroom learning environments that enhance learning for ELLs,
- Writing lesson plans that ensure optimal engagement of ELLs,
- Planning small-group configurations that include ELLs in mainstream instruction,
- Teaching vocabulary in a way that helps ELLs understand content area information,
- Designing reading and writing instruction that is at the appropriate English language level for ELLs,
- Assigning homework and developing assessments that are linked to instruction, and
- Learning to effectively communicate with the parents of ELLs.

Each chapter opens with a classroom scenario that depicts a common challenge in elementary, middle, and high school content area classes, followed by specific ideas for modifying instruction for the benefit of ELLs. These opening scenarios are situated in science, math, and social studies classes. Small-group configurations can be used in all classes.

CHAPTER ONE

Creating an ELL-Friendly Learning Environment

Middle school social studies teacher Ms. Morales was teaching a unit on the settling of Plymouth Colony in the 1620s. She had four ELLs in her class at varying stages of English language acquisition, all of whom had the ability to converse socially with their peers in classroom situations. Ms. Morales wasn't sure why one of her ELLs, Tuan Li, was still in an ESL class, as his oral participation was strong. He spoke well and seemed to follow the lessons.

The goal of the day's lesson was for Ms. Morales's students to be able to demonstrate three differences between the houses of settlers in 1620 and houses in the present-day United States. Ms. Morales wrote this objective on the board. Below it, she also wrote three brief statements about what her students would do during the day's lesson: First, they would take notes about the houses in Plymouth. Second, they would write facts about the houses. Third, they would synthesize their notes and write a paragraph comparing the homes of 1620 with those that exist today.

At the beginning of the lesson, Ms. Morales reviewed the voyage of the *Mayflower* and the first winter of the new settlers in Plymouth, using pictures to retell the story. She observed that her ELLs were able to participate in this oral review and was pleased with their use of the academic language from the lesson. Ms. Morales then introduced the vocabulary from the text that students would read on the Internet. She used pictures to demonstrate the meanings of the words and phrases that she had identified for this lesson, and showed the students how to use a graphic organizer to take notes. She noted that the ELLs in her class appeared to understand the text and were able to write key words in their organizers. However, when Tuan Li wrote his paragraph, he did not transfer the academic language used in the lesson to his writing. Here is what he wrote:

In Plymouth they have small houses with one big rooms. It was only made from straw for the roof and the wooden board for the down part of the house. Houses in river edge, many of the houses is made of brick. The house is big.

Tuan Li had been in U.S. schools for two years. He spoke English well, volunteered in class, and worked cooperatively with classmates. Ms. Morales was pleased with Tuan Li's participation in the oral part of the lesson and with his understanding of the material that he read online, but she became concerned with his writing. She wondered if he really acquired the academic language and concepts of the lesson. His use of academic vocabulary, grammar, and sentence structure was poor. Ms. Morales thought that Tuan Li had been in the United States long enough to acquire the skills necessary to write in English.

* * *

Teachers of ELLs, such as Ms. Morales, should routinely consider the following questions: How long does it take to learn

English? What should we expect during this learning process? What should we do to help students to learn English as they learn content? Title VI of U.S. federal law describes competency in English as the ability to do ordinary classroom work in English and requires schools to provide ELLs with an education that is available to all students in the same system (Alexander & Alexander, 1985). Each state draws from this federal definition to regulate the laws governing the education of ELLs in public schools.

The phrase "ordinary classroom work"—meaning what we expect students to be able to learn in English—is a good starting point for us to think about how to modify classroom instruction. The way we work with ELLs reflects our beliefs about their ability to perform ordinary classroom work. If Ms. Morales mistakenly believes that an ELL is defined as a student who does not speak English, then she might think that Tuan Li is competent in English because his listening and speaking skills are strong. However, the capacity to do ordinary classroom work in English includes the ability to communicate appropriately in social and academic situations by listening, speaking, reading, and writing.

Language Acquisition Versus Language Learning

The term "English language learner" refers to students who have learned a language or languages other than English during their preschool years and are now learning English as an additional language. School-age ELLs like Tuan Li must learn English because they cannot succeed in school without it.

Learning a language is distinct from acquiring it (Krashen, 1982). Consider Tuan Li: He was in the 4th grade when he enrolled in a New Jersey elementary school. He learned English while also learning math, science, social studies, art, music, and physical education. By contrast, he acquired his native language through the process of communicating with his family and community. Acquiring language is an unconscious process, whereas learning a second language is a conscious one (Krashen, 1982). When learning a second language, students must learn about its structure and appropriate use. An ELL whose native language is Spanish, for example, will be accustomed to placing adjectives after nouns, and must learn to do the reverse in English.

Stages of Second-Language Acquisition

Language learning is a developmental process, each stage of which represents growth and expansion of the ability to know, use, and critically think in the new language. The following descriptions of the stages of second-language acquisition are intended to help teachers ensure that their lessons complement the current stage of a student's English learning.

Stage 1: Starting

In this preproduction stage, students are just beginning to acquire a receptive vocabulary. They can listen attentively to explanations supported by visuals, point to correct answers, act out information, draw and label pictures, and understand and duplicate gestures and movements to show comprehension. Some may even be able to copy words from the board. Choral reading and Total Physical Response, a teaching method that encourages ELLs to respond to language with gestures and body language, will work well with students at this stage, who will need much repetition of English words and phrases in context. Students in Stage 1 will also benefit from having a "buddy" who speaks their language. Teachers should focus attention on listening comprehension activities and on helping students to build a receptive vocabulary. It is common for students to listen much more than speak at this stage and to display understanding through body language, such as by pointing to an object. Remember that the school day is exhausting for these newcomers as they are overwhelmed by listening to a new language all day long.

Stage 2: Emerging

Students enter this early production stage when they have been learning English for about six months to a year and are beginning to produce language. During this stage, students can usually speak in one- or two-word phrases, learn new academic vocabulary with visual support, answer yes/no or either/or questions, provide names of items, categorize information, make lists, and write very simple sentences to go with pictures. Students in Stage 2 should begin to participate in whole-class activities. Teachers should aid learning with graphic organizers, charts, and graphs and begin to foster writing in English through labeling and composing short sentences.

Stage 3: Developing

At this stage, ELLs will begin to communicate using short phrases, understand modified content material, match content area vocabulary to definitions, and comprehend their teacher's clearly articulated explanations and directions. They also may begin to initiate social conversations with classmates. Students in Stage 3 will benefit from the use of flashcards and duet and choral reading activities.

Stage 4: Expanding

English language learners at this stage are becoming more fluent. They can highlight important information in a text, use graphic organizers independently, and skim material for specific information; they are also able to analyze, create, debate, predict, and hypothesize in English. However, the writing of ELLs in Stage 4 will still have many errors as the students continue trying to master the complexity of English grammar and sentence structure. The teacher's focus at this stage should be on student comprehension and writing.

Stage 5: Bridging

At this stage, ELLs can perform in all areas close to the level of their native English-speaking classmates. However, they will continue to need teacher support with oral and written use of more complex vocabulary and sentence structure, and may also need support developing learning strategies and study skills. It is important to remember that although students at this stage are no longer in ESL programs, they will still be learning English for years to come.

Building Connections

In the mid–20th century, several scholars contributed to what we know about how languages are learned in the classroom. Current theories pay particular attention to what occurs in the brain during the learning process; see, for example, Sylwester and Cho (1992), Caine and Caine (1991), and Diaz Rico and Weed (2006). Most researchers on the subject believe that the primary function of the brain is to build connections between new information and what it already knows. This biological process is the cornerstone of our knowledge about second-language learning. It suggests that students are not empty vessels of knowledge; rather, they come to class with a body of knowledge that is based on their personal, cultural, linguistic, social, and academic knowledge. When students are engaged in an atmosphere that helps them to build connections to their varied backgrounds across the curriculum and in a welcoming, nonthreatening way, learning is optimized.

According to Krashen (1981, 1982), learning a second language requires the following three core elements:

1. A comfortable learning environment with a low threshold for anxiety
2. Meaningful tasks that purposely engage students to learn how to speak, listen, read, and write in the new language
3. Engagement in tasks that are just a bit beyond the students' current ability

Language Learning and Culture

Learning a language also involves learning the norms of the culture in which the language is used. Routine tasks can pose unique challenges for ELLs if they have not learned these norms. For example, in many U.S. public high schools, students elect class officers—a democratic process. The act of voting in a school election requires students to understand the principles of democracy and elections, as well as what role each class officer plays. Teachers must provide explicit instruction for ELLs to actively understand what it means to be a learner in the classroom community and to participate meaningfully in it.

Social Language Versus Academic Language

Jim Cummins, a renowned scholar of second-language development, believes that language learners engage in social conversational skills before they engage in academic skills (1981, 1984). He posits that students develop basic interpersonal communicative skills through the process of engaging in informal settings such as the school playground or cafeteria. However, to perform successfully in school, students must also attain cognitive academic language proficiency (CALP)—that is, the ability to manipulate language for academic purposes. The amount of time it takes for students to become proficient in a language depends on their backgrounds. Students who have had prior schooling and rich literacy experiences (including a literacy-rich home environment) tend to become communicatively competent in three to five years, whereas those who have previously had limited or interrupted instruction or a radically different type of schooling may take five years or more. Learners who are not fully literate in their native language will take even longer to acquire CALP in the second language.

We do not believe that students learn social language before academic language, as this would imply that learning is a linear process. Both types of learning are optimized when teachers connect new information to students' personal, cultural, linguistic, social, and academic backgrounds (Diaz Rico & Weed, 2006; Echevarria, Vogt, & Short, 2008).

Teachers of ELLs should be attracted to working with such students and create an environment in which students' personal, cultural, linguistic, social, and academic experiences are seen as rich resources. Similarly, ELLs must be attracted to learning in their new environment and interested in learning about the culture in which they now find themselves. Consider the example of Dmitry, a brilliant student who had been at the top of his class in Russia. When his parents decided to come to the United States, he felt very angry about the decision but had no way to express this anger directly to his parents. Instead, he simply refused to try to learn in school. When pressured, he had a cousin do his homework. In short, by refusing to open up to the new language and culture, Dmitry lost a whole year of English language acquisition when he first came to the United States.

Designing Socially Relevant Learning Activities

We believe that students learn best when the curriculum is socially relevant and when students are given opportunities to examine their world, such as in the earlier example of Ms. Morales engaging her students in comparing their lives to the lives of children from the 1620s. Socially relevant curriculum has been found to be an important element for learning (Luke, 1994; Vasquez, Muise, Adamson, & Heffernan, 2003).

Lessons that allow ELLs to participate more fully in their schools and communities should be at the heart of the work of teaching.

Let us return to the example of Ms. Morales's class. Once Ms. Morales began to understand more about the sociocultural realities of her ELLs as well as their language and content learning needs, she adjusted her lessons. Most of Ms. Morales's students played in community baseball games after school. Because she knew that her ELLs were not familiar with baseball and were not being included in the games, she decided to expand the study of the Plymouth settlers to include a comparison of popular games in the colonial United States with those that are popular today. She posted the objectives of the lesson on the board, used a graphic organizer to support her students' learning, and engaged her students in a variety of paired discussions about the two time periods. She also used class time to ask her English-fluent students to encourage ELLs to participate in baseball games after school and to support them when they did.

Characteristics of an Effective Learning Environment

Learning activities must be based on deliberate and explicit instruction that allows multiple opportunities for

- Student understanding of the lesson's key content goals and activities;
- Teacher modeling of activities before students engage in them;

- Frequent opportunities for students to practice activities comfortably; and
- Multiple and repeated connections to student's personal, cultural, linguistic, social, and academic experiences.

Posting Core Content Ideas

As Wiggins and McTighe (2005) note, it is important to plan learning experiences that are based on the core content ideas that we want our students to learn. It is very helpful to post these ideas on the board for student reference, as they not only can provide an anchor for students throughout the course of a unit but also provide teachers with an important reference point when designing and delivering lessons. Posting core content ideas in the form of questions can be particularly helpful, furthering students' interest by encouraging them to seek answers.

Thinking that the terms "reflect" and "belief system" would be difficult for students to understand, Ms. Morales revised her core question to read, "How did the everyday activities of the settlers show what they believed?" She thought that this core question would be more easily understood by all of her students and serve as an important reference point for learning the core concepts.

Posting Daily Content and Language Objectives

The Sheltered Instruction Observation Protocol, also known as the SIOP model (Echevarria et al., 2008), points to the importance of posting daily content and language objectives for our students. Teachers should inform students of the lesson's purpose by sharing with them what material they hope they will learn and what they will be expected to do to learn it.

Teachers should inform students of the lesson's purpose by posting one or two short, student-friendly statements or questions (e.g., "What games did the settlers play in 1620, and what games do we play today? How are they the same and different?"). These statements are intended to focus student attention on the content to be learned and its connection to the overarching unit objective.

Teachers should also provide a list of the key activities that students will do in class that will require them to listen, speak, read, and write. We suggest that these activities be described using action verbs (e.g., "Identify four games that settlers played"). Suggested action verbs for describing listening, speaking, reading, and writing activities may be found in Appendix 1. Activities should be listed in the sequence in which they are to be performed. No more than four key activities should be included.

Ms. Morales began posting her daily content and language objectives on the board before each lesson and read them aloud to her students. She also referred to them throughout the lesson. Presenting objectives visually is essential when teaching ELLs.

Teaching Vocabulary Explicitly

Every subject has its own language and includes thousands of words that are specific to it (Marzano & Pickering, 2005). In science class, for example, an experiment involves making and testing a hypothesis, observing the test, and collecting and analyzing data. Students must learn the academic vocabulary that is required for each subject. Teachers must explicitly teach and display vocabulary in class, as well as identify key terms, words, idioms, and phrases (Debbie calls them TWIPs) that are needed to learn and engage with the subject matter.

Implementing Participation Structures That Support High-Level Active Learning

Learning occurs best when teachers provide students with frequent opportunities to participate and interact with others (Cohen, 1994; Echevarria et al., 2008; Faltis & Hudelson, 1998). Paired work and group work are the most effective methods for engaging students in using language, as they allow students to practice using new content vocabulary in the safety of a small learning community.

In this chapter, we described an effective learning environment for ELLs. We discussed the ability to do ordinary classroom work and outlined the states of English language acquisition. In the next chapter, we will investigate how teachers can plan lessons that will optimally engage ELLs.

CHAPTER TWO

Lesson Planning
to Ensure Optimal
Engagement of ELLs

2

Mrs. Sokolov, a 9th grade social studies teacher, began a unit of study that corresponded with her state's curriculum standards requiring students to understand the role of citizens in a participatory democracy. She introduced the unit by engaging her students in an exploration of the civil rights movement. In planning the first day of the unit, Mrs. Sokolov gathered several articles that she had collected about President Obama, most of which mentioned the fact that he was the first African American to become president. Mrs. Sokolov figured that the best way to begin the unit was to read one of the articles aloud and ask her students to share their opinions about it. She jotted this idea down in her planning notebook. She planned to finish the opening lesson by asking students to identify key words that they would use to describe the significance of President Obama's racial background. This would be followed with a homework assignment to read a chapter from the course text about civil rights and prepare a list of related vocabulary words.

Thinking that her first-day lesson plan was complete, Mrs. Sokolov went to the teacher's lounge for a cup of coffee. While there, she told one of the school's ESL teachers, Ms. Tedesco, how she planned to introduce the civil rights unit. In response, Ms. Tedesco said, "Have you thought about the students who have never experienced what it means to live in a democracy? Many of your ELLs come from countries that are not democracies."

*   *   *

When creating activities to help ELLs connect to content, teachers should be sensitive to U.S.-specific elements that may seem unfamiliar to students from different cultures. We often take for granted that our students have prior knowledge about various people, places, things, and events. If a teacher has not activated prior knowledge or built background information about content material, teaching the vocabulary that is associated with the new content will not solve the problem. Just because ELLs may be able to read words doesn't mean they will understand their meaning in the context of the content being taught. Indeed, many of the ELLs in Mrs. Sokolov's social studies class were not familiar with the democratic process, let alone the specific language and content associated with it. The essential question that the school faculty had chosen for the year was, "What does it mean to live in a democracy?"

At first, Mrs. Sokolov thought that teaching her students about the uniqueness of having the first African American president was a good plan. However, when she began thinking more deeply about the key purpose of her task, she realized that it involved much more than understanding and being able to use vocabulary associated with fighting for one's civil rights. She thought carefully about what it was that she wanted her students to learn. She developed a guiding question that she would post for her students: "How do civil rights affect your life?" By organizing her unit around this question, Mrs. Sokolov believed that she would be able to create and deliver lessons that would require her students to learn about the historical time period of the civil rights movement, and she felt that her guiding question related well to the school's essential question.

We believe that adequate lesson planning must include the following steps:

1. Thinking about what we want students to learn,
2. Identifying methods of assessing student learning,
3. Identifying and addressing ELL-specific challenges inherent to the lesson,
4. Deciding how to activate prior knowledge and build background knowledge, and
5. Designing ways to explicitly guide ELLs as they practice using new language and content.

Teachers also need to think about the visual aids that will best aid comprehension, how to simplify the language of instruction, and how to deliver instruction that is targeted to both the English proficiency levels of students and their grade-level content.

Thinking Backward

Researchers Wiggins and McTighe (2005) point to the importance of "thinking backward"—that is, considering what it is that we want students to learn and how to assess it when planning learning experiences. When Mrs. Sokolov began to plan her lessons, she decided to change her guiding question from "How do civil rights affect your life?" to "What is a civil right?" to ensure that her ELLs understood the concept. Each of the activities that she designed was for the purpose of helping students answer this core question. She also began to think more deeply about the term "civil rights" and the ways in which she might modify the language of her lesson for ELLs without diluting the material. The more she planned, the more she realized that her lesson would be stronger for all of her students.

Specific Content Area Challenges for ELLs

Here are some of the distinct challenges in different content areas that ELLs face and that teachers should consider when planning lessons.

Reading

Many ELLs lack content area vocabulary and have limited comprehension skills in English. Although they may be able to sound out words phonetically, they may not be able to ascertain meaning from the context. English contains many idioms and figurative expressions that may be overwhelming to ELLs. Furthermore, the cultural background depicted in the text may be unfamiliar to ELLs.

Writing

Because many ELLs write through the filter of their native language, word order, sentence structure, and paragraph organization in English may be problematic. There are a plethora of exceptions to the rules in English grammar. In addition, students often lack the vocabulary that they need to successfully write in English.

Mathematics

It is important to remember that mathematical concepts are not necessarily universal. Math teachers need to validate the foreign systems of mathematics and prior mathematical knowledge that ELLs bring to their classrooms. Students may not show work in addition, subtraction, multiplication, and division, or may show such work in a different way. Concepts such as the Fahrenheit temperature scale and U.S. currency units may be unfamiliar to many ELLs. Teachers should also keep in mind that many cultures use commas where we use periods and periods where we use commas; for example, "1,067.32" would be written "1.067,32" in many countries around the world.

Science

English language learners may lack familiarity with the "hands-on" approach to teaching science that is common in the United States. Making predictions and drawing conclusions independently may also be difficult for ELLs. In addition, the vocabulary of science presents a difficulty to students who speak languages where there are no cognates. Directions often involve multiple steps and can consequently be difficult to understand. Science textbooks, which feature complex sentence structures and passive voice, can also prove challenging for ELLs.

Social Studies and U.S. History

Social studies and U.S. history may be the most challenging content areas for ELLs, who may have very limited background knowledge to activate. As with science, textbooks will often contain an overabundance of complex sentences, passive voice, and pronouns. Students may also be unable to tell what is important in the text. Even maps have a nationalistic or cultural focus: In China, for example, the continent of Asia is in the center of the map and China appears larger than it does on U.S. maps.

Language and Content Objectives

Echevarria and colleagues (2008) point to the importance of coming up with both language and content objectives for lessons to let students know what they are expected to learn. *Language objectives* refer to the specific vocabulary or use of language that teachers want their students to learn and use during a lesson. An activity related to a language objective might be as simple as, "Write two key ideas that your partner shares with you." For ELLs, the act of writing ideas must be taught explicitly. *Content objectives* refer to the subect matter information that you want students to know by the end of the lesson.

Mrs. Solokov wrote objectives for the entire unit in her planning notebook and shared them with students on a handout. During the unit, she wrote each day's language and content objectives on the board. For example:

> *Content objective:* Today we will understand what a civil right is by listening to Martin Luther King Jr.'s "I have a dream" speech.

> *Language objective:* Today we will write down three civil rights that are mentioned in Martin Luther King Jr.'s "I have a dream" speech.

Connecting Content to Students' Prior Knowledge and Experience

To help students to meaningfully understand and express their understanding of the content, it is important to connect the lesson's core ideas to students' prior knowledge and experiences. Mrs. Sokolov's revised plan includes asking ELLs to discuss with their parents the kind of government and rights that people have in their home countries. Her plan also includes modeling the interview process. Modeling the tasks that we assign and engaging in think-alouds benefits ELLs greatly, as does guided practice. Many ELLs are not familiar with the step-by-step process of completing a task in a U.S. classroom. When Mrs. Sokolov jots down her think-aloud plan in her planning notebook, she notes the steps that she will model with her students as she prepares for the interview.

Supplementary Materials

Teachers should identify and compile any supplementary materials for their lessons in advance. Although Mrs. Sokolov had many newspaper articles about President Obama, she had not assembled materials about the various types of inequality that her students could discuss. She went to the guidance counselor to learn more about where her students had attended school and lived, then researched and found several Web sites about the types of political ideologies common to these areas. She also selected Web sites that contained news clips from various important events in the fight for civil rights.

It is important to visually display both the language and content goals of the lesson. Goals should be written on the board, on chart paper, or on handouts. If they are written simply, they can greatly assist students. It is also a good idea to include pictures that realistically depict what is to be learned.

Field Trips

Some teachers take their students on field trips to see and experience the content, often as a culminating activity at the end of a lesson. We suggest scheduling field trips for the very beginning of a unit instead, so that students can draw from the experience later. A good example is the teacher who takes students on a trip to a nearby garden, where she helps the students pick weeds. Upon returning to the classroom, the students staple their individual plants onto a piece of cardboard and begin labeling the parts.

Open-Ended Questions

We believe that turning the core ideas that we want students to learn into open-ended questions and posting them on the board is an important aid for learning. Such visual representations are critical, because spoken language is fleeting; once we speak, our words can no longer be retrieved. Posting the core ideas as questions allows students to refocus, revisit, and rethink what is occurring. Mrs. Sokolov posted the following question in her room: "Are civil rights important in a democracy?"

Graphic Organizers

Graphic organizers offer students an important visual for examining the lesson's core ideas. We suggest that teachers use the same graphic organizer for similar tasks. A flowchart, for example, is used for describing a sequence of events. We also believe that all teachers in a particular grade level should use the same graphic organizers. Using similar graphic organizers throughout the school really helps ELLs comprehend the task at hand.

Planning Assessment

When planning lessons, teachers must think about the formative and summative assessments that they will use to determine that students are learning key ideas. In Mrs. Sokolov's case, she also needs to ensure that the language that she uses in her assessments matches the English proficiency levels of her ELLs. (See Chapter 7 for helpful information on creating effective assessments.) It is essential to know the level of English proficiency of each ELL in the class and create learning activities and assessments to match it. As noted in the previous chapter, these levels range from beginners with little to no proficiency to students who are nearly proficient.

Providing Multiple Practice Opportunities

Margarita Calderon (2007) suggests that students need multiple practice opportunities to truly "own" new vocabulary. It is our experience that students need at least 20 repetitions, if not more. To this end, Mrs. Solokov included paired and group work in her lesson plan, which she believed would help her students to practice the interview skills that they were to use at home. She wrote the group activities that she had come up with for the entire unit in her notebook and provided her students with a handout of the activities. Here is an example of a group activity that Mrs. Solokov designed:

Each group will

- Create a short skit about one important event that occurred during the civil rights movement.
- Find or draw illustrations depicting this event.
- Create a list of the key terms, words, idioms, and phrases (TWIPs) that will be used during the skit.
- Prepare to teach the vocabulary before presenting the skit.
- Present the skit to the class.
- Listen to other groups' skits and provide them with feedback based on whether the event was clearly described and key TWIPs were identified and displayed.

After completing her lesson plan, Mrs. Solokov reviewed it one more time to ensure that it was suitable for the various proficiency levels of her ELLs, ensured that the material would be explicitly taught, and provided a range of direct examples of how she wanted her students to use language to express understanding.

*   *   *

We suggest that classroom and subject area teachers complete the checklist in Figure 2.1 and the worksheet in Appendix 2 to help them modify lessons for ELLs. These modifications will benefit all of the students in the class.

In this chapter, we reviewed various planning strategies that are essential to teaching ELLs in the content area classroom. We discussed identifying core ideas and posting them in the classroom, tapping background knowledge, preparing visuals to use during the lesson, using think-alouds, and creating small-group configurations. We also discussed the importance of providing students with multiple practice opportunities to think and learn. In the next chapter, we will further discuss how teachers can use small-group configurations to help ELLs learn academic content.

Figure 2.1
Checklist for Modifying Lesson Plans for ELLs

- [ ] Plan resources, visuals, and vocabulary activities in advance.
- [ ] Act out vocabulary words and key concepts.
- [ ] Use visuals (pictures, videos, drawings, maps) to aid comprehension.
- [ ] Provide a study guide at the beginning of the unit.
- [ ] Identify content and language goals and write them on the board for students.
- [ ] Use graphic organizers.
- [ ] Simplify your language: repeat, restate, reword.
- [ ] Arrange for students to work in groups.
- [ ] Explicitly teach vocabulary and provide students with word walls.
- [ ] Provide multiple opportunities to practice new vocabulary.
- [ ] Add a word bank to activities and tests.
- [ ] Give both written and oral instructions.
- [ ] Teach ELLs to underline or highlight main ideas in text.
- [ ] Assign a buddy to ELLs and arrange for tutoring.
- [ ] Modify instruction so that ELLs can participate in content area lessons.
- [ ] Tailor assignments to ELLs' levels of English language acquisition.
- [ ] Modify tests (e.g., by using word banks, simplifying language, asking fewer questions).
- [ ] Allow ELLs to show what they know in multiple ways (e.g., through oral responses, drawing, labeling, acting out answers).

CHAPTER THREE

Small Group Work and ELLs

Students in Mrs. Mahoney's 6th grade science class were deeply engaged in their assignment as they worked together in heterogeneous groups. The class included six ELLs at various levels of language acquisition and from several different language backgrounds. The students were studying the formations of different kinds of volcanoes. Their assignment was to fill in a chart asking for specific information about each type of volcano.

The ELLs held roles in their respective groups (e.g., artist, time-keeper, errand runner, researcher) that were commensurate with their levels of English proficiency. In one group, Eduardo, an ELL at the emerging state, served as the artist, drawing illustrations of the various types of volcanoes with the support of his group members. In another group, Safwon, a new learner of English, served as errand runner, gathering and distributing all of the supplies from an illustrated list. It was also his job to ask the teacher for help when it was needed. In a third group, Ji Sook, who was at an intermediate stage of English language acquisition, served as the researcher, tracking down information and pictures of various types of volcanoes on the Internet. She printed out the online material and gave it to her group members. Mrs. Mahoney circulated from group to group, monitoring student participation and ensuring that the groups were on task.

Throughout the course of Mrs. Mahoney's class, ELLs were promoted to more English-intensive roles in their groups as their language ability increased. Ji Sook, for example, had only recently been promoted from artist to the role of researcher. In every case, the ELLs' designated roles and tasks were integral to their groups' assignments.

According to Ji Sook, her experience in Mrs. Mahoney's science class was the first time after two years in a U.S. school that she felt comfortable working with her English-fluent peers. Judie, the coauthor of this book, taught in the same school at the time and noticed that all of the students in her 6th grade ESL class had started to work much more in earnest. They began bringing their science work to her class for extra help because they wanted to do a good job in their groups. It seemed clear to Judie that the ELLs in Mrs. Mahoney's class had blossomed and were now much more motivated to learn science.

Not all small-group configurations, however, are created equal. Just because students are working in small groups does not mean that they are cooperating. Let's look at another example in a classroom down the hall.

Students in Mr. Russell's 10th grade biology class worked in small groups to complete an activity sheet with 10 questions and a chart. The assignment was not modified in any way for the benefit of ELLs; there were no visuals, and new vocabulary was not explained prior to the lesson. Many of the ELLs were placed together in a single group, so the groups were not linguistically balanced. Some students worked with their groups, but many broke off into pairs. Students had their own individual activity sheets but were directed to work together to complete them. There were no assigned roles, and the native English speakers often supplied the answers to ELLs without helping them to understand the information. The classroom was noisy and disorganized. Mr. Russell did not circulate among the groups to answer questions or monitor whether the teams were on task. Students were assessed individually and consequently did not support each other's learning, because they had no stake in the group's success.

*   *   *

Research has shown how important cooperative learning is to the academic and social learning of students in general (Cohen, 1994; Echevarria et al., 2008; Radencich & McKay, 1995; Slavin, 1991; Zacarian, 1996). We believe that cooperative group instruction is especially helpful for teaching ELLs.

Some teachers use cooperative learning minimally because they are not sure how best to assess individual student performance when students work in groups. Other teachers believe that cooperative learning reduces their authority in the classroom and makes it harder for them to manage their students. After all, group work requires students to collaborate effectively with peers without their teacher directly supervising every little interaction. It also requires that teachers believe that their students need to talk to learn; as such, it requires a high level of individual and group cooperation (Cohen, 1994).

Group work is based on two premises: that everyone has something important to say, and that everyone is a rich resource, so it is important to listen to all ideas. Mr. Russell's minimal use of this essential strategy significantly limits student practice of English and content; by contrast, Mrs. Mahoney's maximal use of practice can open important and much-needed space for learning language and content. Applying the cooperative learning strategy well involves paying focused attention to the elements outlined in this chapter. Doing so will dispel any concern about assessment and authority.

Taking Cultural Expectations and Belief Systems into Account

Teachers must consider the cultural expectations and belief systems of students when planning group work. Whereas the United States places a high value on individualism—that is, "individual responsibility for self, independence, self-reliance, self-expression, self-esteem, and task over process" (Rothstein-Fish & Trumbull, 2008, p. 9)—70 percent of the world's cultures value collectivism more (Triandis, 1989). For example, in many Asian countries, schools place a strong emphasis on the importance of group harmony. The proverb "The nail that sticks out is hammered down" represents this value. A belief in group work requires us to accept that our students learn best when they learn together.

Arranging the Classroom Space for Active Student Participation

The seating arrangement in the classroom should facilitate paired and small-group learning. Students should be able to easily interact in a face-to-face manner. Arranging desks so that students can see each other in groups of four (or five, if the class is odd numbered) helps ELLs to feel that they are integral to the classroom community. We feel strongly that ELLs should not constantly be pulled aside for separate instruction. Yes, they will need more scaffolding and more teacher attention, and they should certainly receive support from an ESL or bilingual teacher, but they should not be excluded from group configurations.

Emphasizing the Importance of Group Work

Students benefit from working with classmates from varying world, personal, cultural, and linguistic backgrounds, so cooperative learning benefits both ELLs and native English speakers. However, teachers should not expect their students to engage in cooperative learning simply because they are grouped; rather, they should let the students know from the outset that they will be expected to work in groups composed of culturally and linguistically diverse members.

Teaching Students How to Work Cooperatively

Students need to be specifically taught group work skills as well as terms and phrases related to group work, such as "share ideas" and "everyone must take a turn." The latter should be posted for student reference. Conflict among group members should not be viewed as a negative if students are willing to examine their differences, as this process may help them to understand the content more deeply.

It is acceptable for a bilingual group member to explain directions or concepts to a struggling ELL. Indeed, having a student, teacher, or other staff member around to clarify instruction in an ELL's native language is desirable, as it allows students who are not yet able to learn in English to better understand the material and communicate more actively in the future. If there are a significant number of ELLs in the classroom, the amount of time given to finish tasks should be extended to account for the extra explanation time.

Assigning Group Roles

A group's task is best accomplished by assigning roles to each member, such as researcher, scribe, or artist. It is important to determine which roles are most suitable for ELLs during the lesson-planning stage and to explicitly define and model the roles for students during the lesson. When assigning roles, teachers should consider the English proficiency levels of the ELLs in each group. Students should be made aware that their group's tasks can only be considered completed when each role is enacted. As their English proficiency increases, ELLs should be assigned more language-demanding roles. Roles should also be rotated, as each role requires different language functions.

To ensure that all members of a group are participating actively, the teacher may wish to assign the role of social facilitator to one student per group. The social facilitator is in charge of noting how many times each member of his or her group speaks. In her class, Mrs. Mahoney assigned this role to a member of each group and asked him or her to keep a tally of how many times each group mate spoke. When the groups were done with their discussion, Mrs. Mahoney asked the social facilitators to share their tally marks with their groups.

Figure 3.1 shows an example of a social facilitator's tally sheet from Mrs. Mahoney's class. When the members of this group saw that Tom (the social facilitator) and Julia had spoken much more than the others, they began to think of ways in which they might even out the participation.

Figure 3.1
Social Facilitator's Tally Sheet from Mrs. Mahoney's Class

Ji Sook	✓✓✓✓✓
Safwon	✓✓
Tom	✓✓✓✓✓✓✓✓✓✓
Julia	✓✓✓✓✓✓✓✓✓✓✓✓

Although Mrs. Mahoney's science activity did not require illustrations, she felt that assigning the role of artist to Eduardo was essential for him to participate. Another strategy that Mrs. Mahoney used was to have ELLs at the early stages of acquisition shadow a classmate in a role. Eduardo, in his role as artist, was in reality shadowing the student who was assigned the role of scribe.

Strategies for Engaging Students in Group Work

A variety of strategies can be used to engage students in group work. The following are a few that we have used and found effective.

Showdown

This activity is beneficial for reviewing information before a test. Each group comes up with 10 questions about the topic to be reviewed, and group members collaborate with one another to answer them. Each group then passes its list of questions to another group. One student in each group reads the first question on the list to his or her fellow group members, who write their responses on a sheet of paper or note card. When the reader calls out "showdown," group members show their responses. Group members congratulate those with correct answers and coach those with incorrect responses. The list is then passed on to another group member, who reads the second question; this process is repeated until all questions are answered.

This strategy can be modified so that each group makes up a word bank for ELLs, so that they can participate more actively in the group. This word bank provides possible answers to questions that are written in random order. For example, if the activity were about volcano formations, a group might create a word bank such as the one in Figure 3.2.

Figure 3.2
Sample Word Bank Responses

central vent	crater	Mauna Loa
cinder cones	Crater Lake	Mount Fuji
composite volcano	lava	shield volcano
funnel-shaped	magma chamber	

Round Table

The teacher asks a question or provides students with a direction (e.g., "Name as many insects as you can"). One student in each group writes a response, then passes it on to the student sitting next to him or her, who writes a response as well. The paper is passed around the group until group members have written down as many responses as they can think of. English language learners should be among the first to respond, so that the more obvious responses are not taken before they can have a chance. The group with the most correct responses wins some type of recognition. This strategy is suitable for ELLs at the speech-emergent stage if the responses do not require too much writing and spelling does not count.

Three-Minute Review

The teacher stops during a lesson to allow group members to review the information they have just learned with each other. This strategy gives ELLs a chance to clarify questions and review information within the informal setting of their group. The strategy works best when students are given a particular task to complete and team members discuss and write down the most important things they've learned so far. The strategy is suitable for ELLs at the speech-emergent stage if it is modified to give them more time (e.g., 10 minutes instead of 3).

Think-Pair-Share

This popular cooperative learning strategy can be challenging for ELLs who are unable to speak fluently enough to share their ideas. For such students, the strategy may be modified to include drawing (i.e., Think-Pair-Share/Draw), so that an ELL who is paired with an English-fluent student can draw his or her responses rather than share them orally. When the ELL shares his or her drawings, the partner can then respond orally and help label the drawing.

Talking Chips

This strategy encourages ELLs to participate in group discussions. It also keeps one or two students from dominating the discussion. Each member of the group begins with the same number of chips or tokens. When a student wants to speak, he or she puts a chip in the center of the table. After a group member has used up his or her chips, he or she can no longer speak. Those who still have chips must finish the activity.

Fan & Pick

The teacher divides students into groups of four and provides each student with a note card. Every student in every group writes a question on the assigned topic on his or her card. Then, students in each group call numbers one through four. Student #1 holds the cards, fans them out, and asks Student #2 to pick a card. Student #2 reads the question on the card to Student #3, who has five seconds to think before he or she must answer the question. Student #4 then checks the answer and either praises Student #3 for a correct response or coaches him or her in the case of an incorrect response. The students then change roles and move on to the next question. This strategy is suitable for ELLs at the speech-emergent and intermediate-fluency stages.

Numbered Heads Together

This strategy is great for all ELLs because students brainstorm the correct answer to teacher-generated questions together. In each group, students are assigned a number from one to four. After the teacher asks a question, students are given 10 seconds to think of the correct response. They then huddle in their groups to discuss and agree upon a single answer. The teacher then calls out a number. The student with that number from each group must write down the response on a piece of paper. When the teacher gives a signal, the selected student from each team shows his or her answer. Groups with the correct response get a point.

Jigsaw

This strategy helps students become experts in one aspect of a topic and share their expertise with classmates. In each group, students are assigned a number from one to four. Those with the same number from each group are assigned a subtopic and asked to form an "expert group" to research it and create a short presentation. The teacher may wish to assign the same number to ELLs at similar stages of language acquisition and help their group with the language needed to present their information to their home groups. Their presentation could be in the form of drawings with labels and maps. However, the strategy works just as well if the ELLs are spread out among the groups. In such a case, ELLs at the early stages of acquisition can serve as artists, illustrating their group presentations, while more advanced ELLs can serve as project managers, sequencing events or researching information on the Internet.

Reflection and Self-Assessment

At the end of an assignment, students should reflect on how well their group worked together, how they view their own participation, how much they helped each other, and how the group can work even more effectively. When working with elementary age students, it is helpful to make a chart such as the one in Figure 3.3.

Figure 3.3

Group Work Self-Assessment Chart for Elementary School Students

Name: _____ Role: _____	
Members of my group: _____	
I contributed to the group's work by . . .	
One problem our group had was . . .	
A group member who helped me was . . .	
Next time I think we should . . .	

In this chapter, we have detailed critical aspects of effective small-group configurations in the content area classroom and explained why small groups are so important for teaching ELLs. We have also shown how small-group activities can be modified to include ELLs. In the next chapter, we will discuss the importance of explicit vocabulary instruction for ELLs and discuss activities for providing adequate vocabulary practice.

CHAPTER FOUR

Content Vocabulary Instruction for ELLs

Each year, the students in Mrs. Clark's 6th grade class study natural disasters as part of their science curriculum. Typically, 6th grade teachers launch such lessons by asking their students if any of them have experienced a tornado, earthquake, or other such event, and the students share their experiences. However, because Mrs. Clark's ELLs were not familiar with the vocabulary needed to express themselves clearly in English, she decided to introduce her lesson in a way that would also provide explicit vocabulary instruction. Drawing from Echevarria and colleagues' (2008) work on how to spark student interest, Mrs. Clark decided to begin her unit of study by passing out copies of the following excerpt from L. Frank Baum's *The Wizard of Oz*:

From the far north they heard a low wail of the wind and Uncle Henry and Dorothy could see where the long grass bowed in waves before the coming storm. There now came a sharp whistling sound in the air from the south and as they turned their eyes that way, they saw ripples in the grass coming from that direction also. The house whirled around two or three times and rose slowly through the air. Dorothy felt as if she were going up in a balloon. The north and south winds met where the house stood, and made it the exact center of the cyclone. In the middle of a cyclone the air is generally still, but the great pressure of the wind on every side of the house raised it up higher and higher, until it was at the very top of the cyclone; and there it remained and was carried miles and miles away as easily as you could carry a feather.

Before reading the excerpt out loud, Mrs. Clark provided her students with highlighters and asked them to mark any words that they didn't understand. She believed that reading the excerpt would help her students understand some of the key concepts and terms for the unit on tornadoes, and she also knew that many of her students were familiar with *The Wizard of Oz* in their native languages.

After reading the excerpt aloud, Mrs. Clark asked her students to identify the words that they felt they needed to know. Collectively, the students created a word chart and discussed the meanings of the words using the context, their dictionaries, and an electronic translator. Students scanned pictures and discussed the bolded words in a National Geographic book about tornadoes. They linked the bolded vocabulary to what they had read in the excerpt. Once this activity was completed, Mrs. Clark gathered her students around the classroom computer to watch a video clip of a tornado in progress. Drawing from what they had learned from their discussion of the excerpt and the book on tornadoes, the students spoke excitedly among themselves while watching the video clip, using much of the new vocabulary that they had learned: "Look at the funnel!" "Wow, it's twisting!" "It's going to touch down!" In a discussion about the video afterward, one student exclaimed, "I have never seen a tornado. Tornadoes are a scary disaster!"

After the students viewed the clip, Mrs. Clark asked them to write a description of what they had learned from their reading. Several used descriptive words to illustrate the destruction that they had observed. When this task was completed, Mrs. Clark asked each student to read his or her observation aloud to a partner, who in turn was asked to write down the new vocabulary words that the other student used in his or her description. Because the students knew that their partners were going to be listening for new vocabulary words, they made an effort to use them.

* * *

We believe that teachers should use explicit vocabulary instruction and connect new words to students' prior knowledge and experiences. Children become literate as they secure meaning from the world around them: Context cues, such as the golden arches of McDonalds or the red octagons of stop signs, can be understood by children three years old and even younger. The process of learning from these cues is known as forming an "environment print" (Hudelson, 2001). Young ELLs have had many opportunities to build connections among symbols, words, and meanings, but often in other languages and cultural contexts. Teachers of ELLs must therefore create opportunities and multiple demonstrations for students to learn new concepts and vocabulary in English (Crandall, Jaramillo, Olsen, & Peyton, 2002).

More often than not, ELLs haven't been exposed to the English vocabulary and concepts necessary for comprehending content area material, and teachers tend to draw from materials that represent U.S. culture. Lesson design and delivery must help

ELLs to understand English words in the context of their new culture. For example, ELLs who have never seen snow would be at a distinct disadvantage when learning about the seasons; thus, introducing a lesson on seasons by having students go outside during the first snowstorm of the year or by showing them a video of children playing in the snow would provide such students with firsthand experience and better understanding of the concept.

Explicit Vocabulary Instruction

There are two kinds of vocabulary acquisition: direct and indirect. Direct learning occurs when students are explicitly taught vocabulary for a specific purpose. Indirect learning occurs when students acquire vocabulary by hearing it in school or at home, or by reading. English language learners don't learn much of their vocabulary from indirect learning. At home, many parents of ELLs either don't speak English or have a limited grasp of it; at school, many ELLs don't understand much of the conversation that occurs around them. For example, in Judie's school, announcements are always prefaced by the phrase "Please excuse the interruption." Whenever announcements would come on the loudspeaker, one 3rd grade ESL group would parrot the phrase by chanting "peasexcustheruption," having no idea what was being said.

In many kindergarten classrooms, teachers use signals to communicate specific actions that they want their students to do. One time, Debbie and a group of teachers and researchers wanted to see if the signals had the same meaning for ELLs as they did for native speakers of English. They observed a group of kindergarten teachers who formed the letter *L* with their hands. They also observed a second group who flicked the classroom lights on and off while holding up a hand. Both groups stated that these signals were intended for the same purpose: to have students stop what they're doing, look at the teacher, and listen to what the teacher says. Debbie and her group asked the students what these signals meant. Whereas most of the ELLs thought that the signals meant simply that they should stop what they were doing, most of the English-fluent students understood that the signals meant they were to stop what they were doing and look and listen to their teacher. The kindergarten teachers had failed to explicitly introduce the underlying meaning of their signals in a way that the ELLs could understand.

Students may appear to pick up words easily, such as when they sing the lyrics that they are taught in music class. However, they don't always understand what they are singing unless it is explicitly taught to them at their English language level. Although all students need direct instruction in vocabulary, it is especially imperative for ELLs. They must be provided with strategies for figuring out and remembering new words. Also, they need much more exposure to new vocabulary words than do their English-fluent classmates (August & Shanahan, 2006). English language learners need to learn cognates, prefixes, suffixes, and root words to enhance their ability to make sense of new vocabulary. More importantly, they must be given multiple opportunities to use new vocabulary and practice it repeatedly.

Preteaching Vocabulary and Key Concepts of a Lesson

There are two schools of thought regarding preteaching vocabulary. Those in favor of it feel that the rhythm of a lesson is broken if vocabulary words are explained during the reading of text, whereas those against it feel that they are teaching out of context if they introduce new vocabulary before the lesson begins. It is our belief that essential vocabulary should be pre-taught to ELLs after the key concepts of the lesson have been explained. Too often, teachers use the lesson's "big idea" as a jumping-off point, but it is our experience the ELLs won't even understand the big idea if the key concepts and vocabulary have not been taught.

Teaching Students to Recognize Context Clues

Understanding context clues, such as embedded definitions, pictures, charts, and tables, helps ELLs build the blocks (schema) that they will need to comprehend the text. For example, learning about exercising one's right to vote involves learning about the concept of democracy, as well as learning words and phrases that have more than one meaning, such as "exercise" and "right." Teachers of ELLs must ensure that key words with multiple meanings are not misunderstood.

In one 5th grade U.S. history class that we observed, the teacher, Mrs. Dubois, walked her students through a chapter on the causes of the Civil War before the students read the text. They talked about the key concepts that were noted in the introduction to the chapter and linked these to information gleaned from the previous chapter. They read and listed the bolded words, which Mrs. Dubois asked her students to define using the context of the text. Students worked on defining the vocabulary in small groups. They constructed a T-chart with the headings "North" and "South" and listed vocabulary that pertained to each heading. The class then studied the pictures, charts, maps, and timelines in the chapter and discussed how each of these visuals was tied to the chapter's main idea (the widening of the differences between slave and free states before the Civil War). The visuals and small-group arrangements helped the ELLs learn their vocabulary more effectively.

Learning words out of context, such as from a list of dictionary definitions, is very difficult for ELLs. Words and concepts can easily be misconstrued in ways that are not at all related to the intended meaning. When ELLs memorize the meanings of words on a specific subject matter list, they may not be able to use the words in their own writing or verbal production.

Building Background Knowledge

Teachers should explicitly link content to concepts that students have previously learned as well as to students' life experiences. To do this, teachers must first know what their students have previously learned and experienced. In teaching a unit about natural disasters, for example, teachers might ask ELLs for information about the kinds of extreme weather conditions that are found in their native countries. In Mrs. Clark's classroom, a student from the Philippines found an online video clip about the 1991 eruption of Mount Pinatubo that his grandparents had witnessed. Another student found a video clip about a tornado that had occurred in her home country of Argentina. Showing students how the subject matter relates to their countries of origin leads to a deeper level of exploration and understanding and also lets students feel that teachers and classmates are interested in their prior experiences.

The Three Tiers of Vocabulary

It is important to choose the key terms, words, idioms, and phrases—what Debbie calls TWIPs—that your students need to learn. Too often, the phrases and idioms that we use to teach content are implied rather than directly taught. Beck, McKeown, and Kucan (2002) offer a three-tiered model to teach TWIPs:

- Tier 1 includes basic words or phrases that do not need explanation, are commonly used in everyday conversation, and are familiar to most English-fluent students (e.g., *blue, pencil, chair*).
- Tier 2 includes words or phrases that are used often and included in a variety of contexts but that need explanation because they are more descriptive or precise— *conductor* rather than the Tier 1 *driver*, for example, or *pleased* rather than the Tier 1 *happy*. Calderon (2007) also places such linking words as *so, at, into, within, by, if, then,* and *because* in this category.
- Tier 3 includes words or phrases that are not commonly used, are limited to a particular context, and are not likely to be used outside the classroom (e.g., *photosynthesis, quadratic equation, iambic pentameter*).

In classrooms composed of both English-fluent learners and ELLs, teachers must pay attention to all three of the above tiers. Calderon (2007), Hinkel (2009), and Short, Himmel, and Richards (2009) claim that learners need at least 12 practice opportunities using TWIPs in context before they can fully understand them; mere exposure is not enough.

Using Word Walls

Word walls help teachers visually communicate the words and phrases needed for more efficient understanding of new subject matter, and also provide the practice opportunities that students need to move the TWIPs from short- to long-term memory. We recommend having two "word walls" in your classroom to help students practice their words and phrases: one reserved for Tier 1 and Tier 2 TWIPs and another reserved for content-specific Tier 3 TWIPs. Students should help create the Tier 3 wall by selecting key vocabulary from their textbooks by looking at chapter titles, headings, subheadings, and bolded words. Research shows that learning is more effective when students help select the vocabulary that they need to learn (Echevarria et al., 2008). The words on the Tier 3 wall should change from unit to unit.

Another technique that we have used successfully is the portable word wall. Mrs. Clark used a portable world wall with her students during the tornado lesson (see Figure 4.1). Portable word walls are simply vocabulary lists that students create and keep in their binders, thus allowing each individual student to specifically address his or her particular vocabulary learning

Figure 4.1

Example of a Portable Word Wall from Mrs. Clark's Class

New Words	Old Words with New Meanings	People
tornado		meteorologist
cyclone	funnel	scientist
updraft	mass	storm chaser
Tornado Alley	pressure	
wall clouds	alley	
high pressure		
low pressure		
weather satellite		

Everyday Words to Learn	Weather Words to Review
destruction	cumulous clouds
violent	cold front
extreme	cumulonimbus clouds
damage	warm front

needs. Students can have the list handy when they are doing homework and performing a variety of classroom tasks.

Tablemats may also be used as portable word walls during cooperative work. Small groups composed of both ELLs and English-fluent students can construct poster-size tablemats of subject-matter vocabulary. Each tablemat can remain in place while groups rotate from one table to the next, examining the differences between the mats, using the words on each mat in context, and so forth.

Self-Selecting Vocabulary (Reader's Workshop)

Reader's Workshop is an instructional mode for reading that fosters a love of reading by personalizing instruction for each student. In Judie's school, we observed the Reader's Workshop in Ms. Menzella's 2nd grade classroom, where students collected their own new vocabularies from their reading, wrote them on a chart in the room, and explained to classmates what their words meant. Because the reading materials in the Reader's Workshop were individualized, ELLs were able to participate fully in the instruction. Ms. Menzella contributed some vocabulary terms herself, such as prefixes, suffixes, and root words. Students made personal dictionaries to note the words they want to remember.

Reader's Workshop is especially beneficial to ELLs. Ms. Menzella remarked to us, "My classroom represents a class of diverse learners from various cultural backgrounds and learning abilities. I have watched these learners successfully apply the [vocabulary acquisition] strategies as effectively and easily as any other learner in my classroom. Strategy instruction is always introduced using the gradual release of responsibility. In this way, I am able to support any learner who may require additional support."

Teaching ELLs to Pronounce New Vocabulary

It is important for students to practice pronunciation. We suggest that teachers take time to pronounce each new word for their students and have students repeat and practice using the words in context. Teachers should point out proper names, as well. In one class that we observed, during a lesson on the Civil War, the teacher had students pronounce the names of historical figures and battles without specifically defining the words. At the end of the lesson, one ELL asked, "Is Jefferson Davis a person?"

Students are more likely to use a word in oral discourse if they feel confident of the pronunciation and understand what the word means. Teachers should point out pictures of people and use maps to show places when teaching pronunciation. In Mrs. Clark's class, students practiced pronouncing the names of countries and states as they located them on a map where natural disasters occurred. They also practiced the names of volcanoes. This made it easier for them to discuss and retain the material.

Strategies for Supporting Vocabulary Instruction

During a lesson on the Civil War in Mrs. Wondra's 5th grade social studies class, ELLs could not understand what a blockade was. Mrs. Wondra selected a student and had him wear a sign reading, "English Ship." Then she asked him to leave the room. Mrs. Wondra explained that the English ship wanted to bring food into the Confederate states. She then instructed another student to wear a sign that read, "Union Ship." She asked him to try to prevent the English ship from supplying the Confederate states with food. The "Union Ship" student barred his classmate from reentering the class. Mrs. Wondra told her class that the Union ship had created a blockade. This enactment helped all of Mrs. Wondra's students learn the meaning of a blockade.

*   *   *

According to Howard Gardner's (1993) theory of multiple intelligences, there are many different kinds of intelligences, including linguistic, logical-mathematical, bodily-kinesthetic, musical, interpersonal, and intrapersonal. Broadly speaking, linguistic intelligence involves the capacity to use and manipulate language through listening, speaking, reading, and writing. Gardner notes that this is the intelligence that is measured on standardized tests. Although many ELLs have linguistic intelligence in their native language, they cannot demonstrate it in English. They may not perform well on standardized tests or in classrooms that do not address their language learning needs. We believe that such poor performance occurs when teachers focus solely on linguistic intelligence and emphasize such processes as lecture-driven lessons, student presentations in front of the whole class, and essay writing, all of which require a high level of English comprehension and fluency. In addition, most of the teaching in U.S. schools is geared toward students who prefer to learn by listening and engaging in oral activities and discussions. This type of learning requires skills that ELLs do not yet have when they are learning English.

We believe that learning occurs best when teachers create lessons that are targeted to the various learning styles and multiple intelligences of ELLs. For example, some ELLs are bodily-kinesthetic learners: they can learn better by touching, molding, and holding objects than by listening to lectures. They like to play games, set up experiments, and move around the room. It is our experience that, during the early stages of language acquisition, ELLs are usually visual and kinesthetic learners. Other ELLs might lean more toward interpersonal learning: they like choral reading and group activities and are more likely to act spontaneously and intuitively. In addition to differences in learning styles, ELLs differ in terms of learning background: some are highly literate in their native languages but familiar only with lecture-based lessons; others have had limited formal schooling; and still others have had their schooling interrupted many times.

Mr. Martinez, a 5th grade social studies teacher, introduced a lesson on the growth of cities in the United States by telling a simple story using basic vocabulary that all his students could understand. To further help the visual learners in his class, he illustrated his story as he told it by holding pictures: of a sky-scraper, of an elevator, of Jane Addams, of Hull House in Chicago, of people living in tenements, and so forth. Then, he had students retell the story by following the sequence of the pictures as he held them up. After the lesson, English-fluent students read the textbook and answered questions, while ELLs practiced new vocabulary by using the visuals and listening to a recording that Mr. Martinez had made of the story.

Graphic Organizers

Graphic organizers are visual tools that help ELLs to understand and organize information. They are like mind maps that promote active learning and creativity and help students to develop higher-level thinking skills. Graphic organizers are important tools for converting complex information into manageable chunks, as content materials often contain text that is too dense for ELLs. We believe that all classrooms should use graphic organizers such as webs, diagrams, and charts.

Graphic organizers are also excellent tools for helping students to interpret and summarize text. For example, when Mrs. Lautz's 6th grade students studied a new chapter in their social studies book, they first made a list of all the bolded words, section titles, and proper nouns in the chapter, then categorized them under headings in a simple graphic organizer. Figure 4.2 shows an example of this type of organizer used for an assignment on the Industrial Revolution in the United States. In the first column, students drew a picture or wrote about an invention from the early 1800s. In the second column, they wrote the inventor's name. In the third column, they stated why it was important. The students reviewed the information on their organizers using the following frame:

_____ invented the _____. It was important because _____.

Figure 4.2
**Sample Graphic Organizer for
Lesson on the Industrial Revolution**

Invention	Inventor	Why Invention Is Important

When they were done, the students shared their organizers with a small group of classmates. This small-group activity gave ELLs have the opportunity to use oral language and review vocabulary.

Strategies for Practicing Vocabulary

English language learners should practice new vocabulary every day. During a 6th grade science unit on the solar system, one ESL teacher we know had students draw and label parts of a planet that they themselves made up. The students used their new vocabulary to expand the creation of their imaginary planets. They then had to present their imaginary planets to the rest of the class, thus exhibiting their mastery of academic vocabulary.

Flash cards are particularly helpful for ELLs because they can be tailored to individual levels of language acquisition. One side of a flash card should have a word or phrase written on it, and the other side should have a definition or illustration of the word or phrase. Students can create flash cards during class time. As they learn vocabulary, they can sort their cards into two piles: the words and phrases that they have learned, and the ones that they have not yet learned. Students can be encouraged to take their flash cards home and refer to them when engaged in such tasks as brushing their hair, eating snacks, or riding the school bus. They can even play different games with their flash cards, such as word searches or crossword puzzles. Judie has her ESL students work in small groups to design short vocabulary tests at the end of a unit. Each group comes up with a different test; groups then exchange tests with each other and try to answer the questions. Some of the student-generated tests are more creative and fun for students to take than those a teacher would have made, and they can even be more difficult. The overall purpose of flash cards is for students to internalize and be able to use content-related words and phrases independently and at will.

One of the activities in Judie's school is an annual science fair. Students traditionally prepare their projects for the fair using the scientific method, and they must present their projects via a slide show that includes such scientific terms as *question, hypothesis, materials, procedure, data, results,* and *conclusion.* Here are some other strategies that teachers can use to help their students practice vocabulary:

- **Thumbs-Up!** The teacher says a definition of a vocabulary word. If the students know the word, they raise their hands in a thumbs-up position. The teacher then counts to three, and the students quietly say the word.
- **Find the Word.** The teacher says a sentence but omits a vocabulary word. Each student has a pile of cards with a vocabulary word on each and puts the card with the missing word facedown on his or her desk. On the count of three, the students turn their cards over.
- **Act It Out.** Students take one card each from a pile of cards, each one of which has a vocabulary word on it. One student is chosen to act out the word on his or her card while classmates try to guess what the word is. Whoever answers correctly gets to act out his or her word next.

- **Bingo.** Each student makes a bingo card that features lines of vocabulary words in place of numbers, writing the words in random order so that all of the cards are different. The teacher reads a definition, and students mark the attendant word on their cards. The first student to mark all of the words in a line on the card calls "Bingo!" and becomes the next caller.

- **Beach Ball Vocabulary.** The teacher writes the vocabulary words on a beach ball and asks the students to stand in a circle. The teacher then throws the ball to a student, who reads the word that is under his or her thumb and defines it.

- **Word Search Vocabulary.** The teacher has students create a word search game on graph paper using their vocabulary words. Instead of providing a list of the words to be found, the students list the words' definitions as clues. When they are done, the students solve each other's puzzles.

- **Find the Transition Word!** The teacher asks students to find the transition words (e.g., *because, however, so, and, if*) that link, break, or contrast clauses in a discussion.

Making Vocabulary Stick—Literally

We have found that younger ELLs love using sticky notes, highlighters, Wikki Stix (i.e., wax-coated pieces of yarn), and highlighting tape in class, so any lesson that includes these materials stands a good chance of sparking students' interest. The students in Ms. Menzella's 2nd grade class collected new vocabulary by marking every new word they came across in their textbooks on a sticky note, which they then used to mark the page on which the word is found. We have also seen students learn the conventions of nonfiction text by marking and labeling titles, headings, insets, maps, charts, table of contents, index, and glossary.

Highlighting is an essential strategy for ELLs. We have our students mark new vocabulary and find the meaning in the text using a highlighter in consumable books. For this very reason, we like to use consumable books with our ELLs as much as possible. If students want to highlight words in nonconsumable books, they should use highlighter tape or Wikki Stix. Wikki Stix are reusable, but highlighter tape is not.

Participants in Judie's professional development workshops have told her that their districts buy extra textbooks for ELLs to use. These books are highlighted by the teacher and kept in the classroom library. This is an immense help to ELLs because they can immediately see what is important in the text.

Resources for Teaching Key Concepts and Vocabulary

Teachers may wish to use carefully selected educational TV programs (such as those found on the Discovery Channel), videos from school and town libraries, and Internet resources to introduce units of study. Sixty years of historic news archives from NBC News are now available free for teachers to use in their classrooms at http://www.hotchalk.com. Key academic vocabulary can also be introduced by reading stories aloud, such as in the case of Mrs. Clark's read-aloud from *The Wizard of Oz.*

In this chapter, we explored the importance of direct instruction of vocabulary for ELLs. We examined activities that teachers can use to provide adequate repetition and practice of new vocabulary words and concepts, presented visual and tactile activities that work especially well with ELLs, and noted resources and activities that can be used with the whole class while also benefiting ELLs. In the next chapter, we will examine reading comprehension strategies that are crucial for ELLs to learn.

CHAPTER FIVE

Reading Comprehension Instruction for ELLs

5

Ms. Menzella gathered her 2nd grade students on the rug in her classroom to hear a story entitled *The Doorbell Rang*. She explained to her students that they were going to learn how to make pictures in their heads. "When we make pictures in our heads of what is happening in a story, it is called visualizing," Ms. Menzella explained. In the story, two children are sitting at the dining room table looking forward to sharing a plate of 12 cookies that their mother had baked. At the end of the first page, Ms. Menzella asked the students to draw a picture of the plate of cookies and to think about what kind of cookies they were. After students made their drawings, they examined the picture of the chocolate chip cookies that was on the next page of the book and shared their own pictures with the class. When one of the ELLs, Soon Ji, showed her picture, she sighed, "I was wrong"— she had drawn 12 sugar cookies with red sprinkles. Ms. Menzella explained to the students that mind pictures do not need to be correct. "The pictures in your heads can change when you get new information. A picture is new information," she explained. Ms. Menzella believed that it was especially important to let her ELLs know this, because they are often product oriented and focused on having a correct response.

* * *

As we noted in Chapter 4, Ms. Menzella used the Reader's Workshop approach in her classroom. What we like about using Reader's Workshop with ELLs is that it allows the students to read books that they select themselves and apply strategies that they learn in class to their reading. It's a good idea for teachers to have short minilessons during which they can model comprehension strategies, followed by student practice time (either individually or in pairs) using books at appropriate reading levels. As part of the Reader's Workshop, students should hold individual conferences with their teachers two or three times a week, or more for ELLs.

Teachers should teach ELLs the exact language that they will need to talk about what they have read. We believe that it is highly motivating to essentially tell students, "This is what good readers do, and now you are going to learn how to do it, too." English language learners also reap the benefits of participating in whole-class instruction while also individually practicing with books that are suitable for their levels of English language acquisition.

At the heart of Reader's Workshop are six reading comprehension strategies that we believe are important to teach to ELLs at all different grade levels, regardless of whether the Reader's Workshop approach itself is used:

1. Visualizing what is happening in the story,
2. Activating background knowledge by making connections,
3. Asking mental questions to self-check comprehension,
4. Learning how to make inferences about what is read,

5. Determining the importance of information in a text, and

6. Synthesizing information that is learned.

Visualizing What Is Happening in the Story

In the example at the beginning of this chapter, Ms. Menzella wanted her students to use visualization to help them understand the story she was reading. She checked her students' comprehension by reviewing the pictures that they'd drawn. If the drawings didn't accurately reflect the content of the book, Ms. Menzella would modify her instructional plans to support better comprehension. For example, she might separate the class into small groups of four for the purpose of enacting the story and dividing up 12 chocolate chip cookies.

When Judie first started to teach visualization to her 1st and 2nd grade ELLs, she was reluctant to use the word "visualization," certain that it was too advanced for her students. One day, when talking to a group of 2nd graders about the mental picture that she had in her head, one of her students said, "Oh, you mean visualize." We believe that it is important to teach the ELLs accurate terminology. It is important for ELLs to learn the same vocabulary for discussing their ideas as their classmates.

Activating Background Knowledge by Making Connections

Keene and Zimmerman (1997), Miller (2002), and Harvey and Goudvis (2007) have noted the importance of connecting reading material to background knowledge. Activating students' background knowledge helps students to connect their prior experience, or schema, to the learning material. Of course, the schemas that ELLs bring to the classroom may be very different from those of their classmates. Teachers should help students make three distinct types of connections: text-to-self, text-to-text, and text-to-world.

Text-to-Self Connections

A text-to-self connection is a link that readers make between the text that they are reading and something that has happened in their own lives. This type of connection helps them to comprehend the text and to share their unique schemas with their classmates. English language learners should learn the phrases that help them to frame their thoughts (e.g., "This reminds me of when I . . . ," "My connection helps me to understand the story because . . ."). Drawing text-to-self connections helps students to better understand feelings and behaviors of the figures about which they are reading.

Carolina, a 2nd grade ELL, came to the United States from Costa Rica with very limited English. She received reading instruction in both mainstream and ESL classrooms. One day, her ESL class was discussing a passage in the book *Pa Lia's First Day,* in which someone refers to the main character as "Four Eyes." Here is what Carolina wrote:

> I have a text to self connection. My mom had glasses at 2nd grade. Everyone call her four eyes and they put round things in their eyes to make fun of her. These make me understand how Pa Lia feels.

Although Carolina had only been in the country for six months, she was able to make a text-to-self connection that helped her understand what was happening in the story. By contrast, Armando, a classmate of Carolina's, wrote the following in reaction to the same passage from the book:

> This reminds me of when I got glasses and I broke them. My mom was mad at me.

Whereas Carolina's text-to-self connection helped her to understand how Pa Lia felt, Armando's connection was irrelevant to the story. His response was a good indicator that additional supports were needed to help him to understand the text.

Text-to-Text Connections

Text-to-text connections are links that students make between the text that they are reading and another book that they have read. It is important to teach students the language of text-to-text connections. When Judie visits elementary Reader's Workshop classrooms, she hears phrases such as "This reminds me of another book that I read" and "I have a text-to-text connection." Teachers may find that they need to prompt the use of this strategy with ELLs by asking, "Does anyone remember another book where children had to share with their friends?" or, "This story is about sharing. What else have we read about sharing?" Explicit instruction of the strategy accompanied by a lot of modeling is especially important for ELLs.

Text-to-text connections can be explored by using graphic organizers to compare different books. This can happen at any grade level—elementary school students might chart similarities and differences in different versions of the Cinderella story, for example, or high school students might draw connections between characters from two different Shakespeare plays. Graphic organizers build on our core belief that learning is best accomplished when accompanied by a visual model.

Text-to-World Connections

Text-to-world connections are links that students make between the text that they are reading and something that has happened in the world. When students from other countries make connections with their homelands, they are more likely to learn. This is an important strategy for ELLs because, as with text-to-self connections, they are using their own schema to understand the text. They should be taught to use sentence starters such as "This makes me think about . . . ," "I remember when . . . ," and "This is what happened in my country."

Let's take a look at a student in a 4th grade ESL class where the teacher, Ms. Hernandez, was beginning a science unit on habitats. To jump-start the unit, Ms. Hernandez had put a pile of books on forest habitats at the center of a table. Students were excited to look through the materials: "Look at this!" and "I didn't know this!" they shouted as they examined the books. The students squirmed with excitement as they pointed out items of interest to their classmates.

Junya stopped and studied a picture of a raccoon. "Ms. Hernandez, you won't believe what I see on Japanese TV!" he exclaimed. "They have raccoons in Japan! They make big problem."

"Hey," said Roberto. "That's a connection." He paused and thought for a moment. "Is it text-to-self or text-to-world connection?" After much discussion, the class decided that Junya has made a text-to-world connection.

Asking Mental Questions to Self-Check Comprehension

Good readers are always asking themselves questions before, during, and after reading. Because many of her 6th grade students did not have sufficient background information about the Underground Railroad before the start of a unit, Mrs. Danahy developed a question web with her class and provided her students with picture books and Internet resources, then helped them to use these materials in groups to generate questions and write them on sticky notes. In front of the class was a large chart. Student placed their sticky notes on the left side of the chart; as they found the answers to their questions in their reading, they wrote these down on sticky notes as well and placed the notes on the right side of the chart.

In a 6th grade social studies unit on the Civil War, Mrs. Danahy introduced a lesson on the Underground Railroad using a simple book for students on the subject called *If You Traveled on the Underground Railroad*. She questioned them about the book's title: "I wonder where people traveling on the Underground Railroad in the story will go?" A student immediately asked what the Underground Railroad was. Dmitry, an ELL at the emerging stage of English language acquisition, wondered how a railroad could really be underground. He knew the meaning of the words "underground" and "railroad," but had a lot of difficulty with the concept. By listening to the questions of other children and reading a book at an adequate reading level, he was able to understand much of the work in the classroom.

English language learners will be more likely to ask good questions if they first read books and practice with a buddy or partner. Here are ways to help your students get started:

- Ask students to predict what the story will be about based on the title or picture on the cover.
- Explain that a prediction is a guess—it doesn't have to be correct; it just needs to make sense. Teach students that their predictions might change as they read.
- Help students identify stopping places in the text where they should think of questions or make predictions. Ask them to mark these places with sticky notes or write about them in their reading notebooks.

Differentiated Expectations

Mrs. Danahy had differentiated expectations for participation in her class; students were in the habit of reading different books at different levels about the same topic. For example, one of Mrs. Danahy's ELLs, Daniel, read an entire book about the U.S. Civil War written in Korean. This background information gave him the schema that he needed to participate at some level in the social studies lesson. Because differentiation was the norm in Mrs. Danahy's class, Daniel and Dmitry did not stick out when they read different books about the same topic. They were able to follow much of the class discussion and pose simple questions such as "Why is this family running way?" and "Were the people afraid?" In addition, they were able to participate fully in the ensuing discussion by drawing from Mrs. Danahy's modeling and visualizing examples.

Learning How to Make Inferences About What Is Read

Good readers draw inferences while they read—that is, they "read between the lines"—as much of what authors convey is implied rather than directly stated. English language learners need to learn strategies to infer meaning by making connections to prior knowledge, visualizing, and predicting. Inference is very difficult for ELLs, as they are already struggling with grammar, sentence structure, and vocabulary. Teachers must therefore explicitly teach their ELLs to infer meaning, and relay such helpful framing phrases as "I predict . . . ," "My guess is . . . ," "I think that . . . ," "My conclusion is . . . , " "I infer that . . . ," and so on.

Mrs. Schnee's 1st grade ESL students sat on the rug on a cold winter day. They could see a snow-covered field through a window. Mrs. Schnee held up a book called *The Snowy Day*. She told her students, "When I look at the cover of this book, I can infer that this story takes place in the winter. I infer this because I see snow, just like outside my window." She then asked students to infer what happens in the story from the picture. One student, Karim, said, "I infer that the boy can't play outside for a long time." Karim used the language that he had been taught to describe what he believed occurred in the story. When Mrs. Schnee asked him why he made this inference, Karim replied, "My schema tells me that it is winter and the snow is cold." Mrs. Schnee asked Karim to point out what in the picture made him think that the book was set in winter. Karim pointed to the snow and to the snowsuit that the boy was wearing.

Determining the Importance of Information in a Text

Good readers can distinguish between important and unimportant information in nonfiction text. This ability is key to understanding the content that students must read. First, teachers should introduce students to the conventions of nonfiction text, such as by having them scan chapter titles, headings, subheadings, picture captions, maps, glossaries, and indexes. English language learners should receive plenty of support before they even begin to read the text. They need to understand that reading is not necessarily a front-to-back task.

Students in Mr. Hopkins's 10th grade history class learned to scan the title, table of contents, bolded words, photographs, captions, maps, headings, subheadings, and labels in a textbook chapter to preview information for a unit on immigration to the United States. Even though the text as a whole was above the reading level of some of the ELLs in the class, they were still able to access enough information this way to gain important information about the topic.

Ms. Meldonian was teaching animal adaptations to her 3rd grade science class. She wrote down the key idea of the chapter that the class was reading on the chalkboard: *Adaptations are important to an animal's survival.* She taught her students that relevant information is that which is related to the key idea. She gave several examples of information from the chapter and asked students to practice deciding what is relevant and what isn't. Students then read the chapter. When they were done, Ms. Meldonian divided them into groups and had them brainstorm what they'd learned. Students in each group wrote a list of information they'd learned from the chapter and then placed an *R* next to facts that they feel were relevant. Ms. Meldonian made a large T-chart and displayed the relevant and irrelevant facts from the groups' lists in front of the whole class (see Figure 5.1).

Figure 5.1
Sample T-Chart of Relevant Versus Irrelevant Information

Relevant Information	Irrelevant Information
Animals have different features and behaviors.	Tigers are big animals.
An animal's body part can be an adaptation.	Some adaptations are strange.
	Vampire bats have a funny name.
Adaptations help animals live in their homes.	
Adaptations help animals hide from enemies.	

Synthesizing Information That Is Learned

Good readers know how to summarize important information and incorporate it into their schema. As they read, they carry on an internal conversation, asking themselves what they understand or don't understand, whether they agree or disagree, and what they wonder.

Mrs. Cirigliano taught the students in her 5th grade class to synthesize the information that they read in an expository text about nutrition. She had students work with partners to read the text together. Each pair had to decide how much of the text to read before stopping to review and synthesize information. Most pairs decided to stop after each paragraph. Every time they did so, they took turns sharing one comment about what they had read and responding to their partner's comment. This comment could take the form of a response to the reading, an interesting fact, or a question about the text. Students were encouraged to think carefully about each comment, as they were allowed only one comment at a time. Mrs. Cirigliano modeled the language students could use to make their comments (e.g., "This reminds me of . . . ," "I felt that . . . ," "I didn't understand it when . . .").

Mrs. Dennis tells her 2nd grade students that there are two voices speaking when they read: The voice that they can hear is their speaking voice, and the other is the one inside their heads. This second voice helps them to think about what they are reading.

When students in Mrs. Dennis's class synthesize information, they do more than retell what they have read; they also demonstrate understanding of the reading strategies that they have used. They retell what they have read from two points of view: that of their own experience, and that of the authors or of characters in their reading. True synthesis, however, involves that "Aha!" moment that readers have when they really "get" the text.

Synthesis cannot occur if the reader does not understand the key vocabulary in the text. It requires the reader to make many connections to his or her life in order to find deeper meaning, create mental pictures of what is happening in the story, listen to the voice in his or her head, and ask questions about what the text means.

In this chapter, we examined the six essential reading comprehension strategies that should be taught to ELLs in all grade levels. We discussed how to teach students to visualize what is happening in the text, activate background knowledge by making connections, ask mental questions to self-check comprehension, learn how to draw inferences from the text, determine the importance of information in the text, and synthesize the information. By using these strategies, teachers can help ELLs to become better readers. In the next chapter, we will discuss how to provide ELLs with effective writing instruction.

CHAPTER SIX

Writing Instruction
for ELLs

Yimin was a 4th grade student from China who had been in the United States for three years. She was progressing normally in most content areas but had great difficulty writing. Her classroom teacher, Mr. Klein, referred her to Judie's ESL class because he was concerned about her writing level. He sent Judie the following writing sample, written in response to the question "If you were an animal, what animal would you like to be and why?":

> I like be eagle becas eagle birds king and he fly very up. They scard. When they baby, they take off they feather and they squek they claw.

Judie read Yimin's school records, which indicated that Yimin had been exited from a neighboring school district's ESL program after only two years. Judie began to wonder if Yimin wasn't exited too soon, before she could become a proficient listener, speaker, reader, and writer in English.

*   *   *

Learning to write in English is a developmental process that involves being able to

- Communicate meaningfully through writing,
- Write for a range of purposes,
- Use culturally appropriate terms, and
- Use correct form and grammar.

Teaching ELLs to write in all subject matters is as important as teaching them to speak, listen, and read in English. Teachers must offer students direct instruction in how to write for different content areas—and must also understand the writing challenges that ELLs experience.

Determining the Degree of Writing Instruction That Is Needed

Writing is a particularly challenging language domain for ELLs to master, perhaps due to the lack of intensity and intentionality that we devote to it. In some schools, students are no longer considered ELLs when they have acquired the ability to listen and speak in English. But oral language skills are deceiving; they may make students appear to be much more fluent in English than they are. The ability to learn ordinary classroom work in English means that ELLs must be able to write in English at or near the level of their English-fluent peers.

Teachers should ask the following initial questions to ensure that they are providing adequate writing instruction:

- Are ELLs given multiple meaningful opportunities for bringing their prior knowledge into learning experiences?

- Are ELLs given explicit opportunities to learn how to write appropriately in the content area?
- What supports are ELLs given for expanding their knowledge and usage of terms and phrases?

Let's visit what Sophy Pich had to say about the challenges that he experienced learning how to write in English. A teacher in an after-school writing program for high school ELLs that Debbie led, Pich wrote the following passage to stimulate his students' interest in writing:

It was, I believe, in the 3rd grade that I was first taught to write summaries to books. I was never able to finish the assignments correctly. Most of the time, what I did was go to the sections of the books that I thought that I was understanding and copy paragraphs that seemed important to be included in the summaries onto my paper. I would do that until I felt that I had accomplished summarizing, and then I would write as the last paragraph, "If you want to find out more about this book, you have to pick up a copy of your own." To this day, now a senior in college, I still suffer from English grammatical/pronunciation syndrome. I still am unable to be sure of how to use my verb tenses and structure; is it "has he learnt it?" or "have he learned it?"

Learning to write involves being able to communicate and convey ideas meaningfully. In Pich's case, it was critically important for his teachers to model and conduct a think-aloud about the summary-writing process, as well as to engage him in practicing the process. English language learners need this type of deliberate instruction about writing to learn how to become fluent writers.

Using Conventions from the First Language

Students will often translate words directly from their native language into English using conventions from their native language. Because different languages have their own rules of grammar, student writing often results in errors. For example, a student translating the term "green apple" directly into English from Spanish might write, "apple green," because adjectives follow nouns in Spanish. Yimin's writing sample at the beginning of this chapter is another example of how student writing often obscures the student's intended meaning.

Tips for ELL Writing Instruction

Here are some tips that teachers can use with ELLs at the emerging stage of acquisition.

- Do not expect ELLs to free-write in English. Why teach them to write incomprehensibly? If you do engage ELLs in free-writing, it might be more appropriate to ask them to write in their native languages and then translate what they have written for you.
- Do not have ELLs write journals every night at home unless you are going to be reading the journals regularly. If translation is available, you may wish to have emerging ELLs write in their native languages; otherwise, ELLs should not be writing journals until they are at a more advanced stage of acquisition.

- Do not assign open-ended topics to ELLs (e.g., "If you were an animal, what animal would you want to be and why?").

- Provide students with authentic reasons to write, as well as examples of what you expect and a firm idea of how you will be assessing their writing.

- It is our opinion that ELLs learn to write better if they begin with nonfiction content area topics, as these will include specific vocabulary that they must learn. It is also easier for teachers to differentiate nonfiction writing assignments than fiction ones in mainstream classes. We encourage you to teach writing in all content areas before exposing ELLs to creative writing. Graphic organizers can be used most effectively for teaching nonfiction writing, because they provide students with language chunks that they can then use.

Calkins's Four Phases of the Writing Process

According to Calkins (1994), there are four distinct phases of the writing process: prewriting, writing, editing, and revising. As we explore each phase, we will be looking again at Ms. Meldonian's 3rd grade class, where students were researching forest animals for their science unit on habitats. This was their first research project. We will follow the work of Joseph, who was at the emerging stage of English language acquisition.

Phase 1: Prewriting

Ms. Meldonian first had students brainstorm a list of animals that they thought lived in the forest. She listed the students' ideas in sentence form on chart paper. Then, she asked her class to look for information on the Internet about an animal that interested them from one of the habitats that they had studied. The ELLs in her class could only select articles online that they were able to read. Ms. Meldonian directed Joseph and other ELLs to http://www.enchantedlearning.com, a Web site that posts articles written at levels suitable for ELLs in the emerging stage.

After students printed out their articles, Ms. Meldonian had them brainstorm questions that they wanted answered about their animals. To address her students' various stages of English language acquisition, she created different graphic organizers for each, supplying the questions that they needed to answer on the organizer and modifying the questions for each ELL's level of English language acquisition. Figure 6.1 shows an organizer suitable for Joseph's level of acquisition.

Figure 6.1

Sample Graphic Organizer for ELL Use During the Prewriting Phase

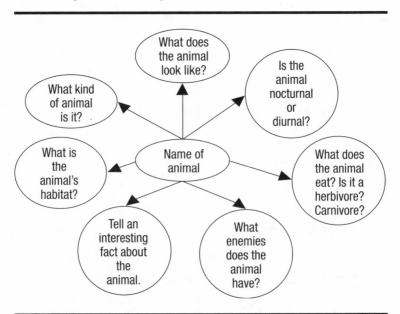

Graphic organizers, charts, pictures, photos, films, field trips, and other visual and auditory experiences are important supports to include at the prewriting stage. Using complete sentences in graphic organizers greatly helps ELLs to learn the language of content. Further, encouraging ELLs to copy sentences down is also helpful.

Ms. Meldonian modeled the type of questions that students should answer in their writing: "The question is 'What kind of animal is it?' Let's see. My animal has fur and drinks its mother's milk, so it must be a mammal." During prewriting, teachers should provide many such think-alouds. Using terms, words, idioms, and phrases (TWIPs) in context is important at this stage, as it strengthens the link between oral and written language. Because many ELLs need to see and experience what they are going to write, teachers should also model the type of writing that they expect to see. Ms. Meldonian asked Joseph the name of his animal and wrote, "This animal is a hedgehog. It is a mammal." Teachers should spend a good deal of time at this stage with new learners of English, showing them multiple samples of the type of writing that is required of them.

Phase 2: Writing

Once students' background knowledge has been activated, the writing phase should commence. Ms. Meldonian asked students to highlight the information in their online articles that they would need to know in order to answer the questions in their graphic organizers. Students did this together in small groups. Ms. Meldonian asked ELLs in the first stage of acquisition to serve as "art experts"—their task was to collaborate with classmates to draw or find pictures of their chosen animals and habitats. At this stage, it is important to display a list of content area TWIPs to which students can refer. Joseph was able to answer five of the seven questions on his organizer, as shown in Figure 6.2.

Figure 6.2
Joseph's Completed Graphic Organizer

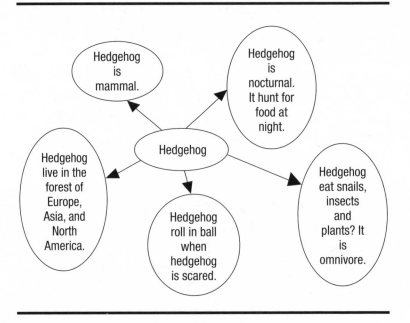

As students acquire more language, they will be able to make their own graphic organizers and write from them. In addition to the graphic organizer, Ms. Meldonian provided Joseph with the following frame for writing:

[Name of Animal]

The name of this animal is [name of animal]. It is a [mammal, bird, or reptile]. It lives in the forests of [continent or country].

[Name of animal] eats [kind of food]. It is [nocturnal or diurnal] because it eats food during the [night or day].

Something unusual about my animal is that _____ _____.

Here is Joseph's draft report:

Hedgehog

The name of this animal is hedgehog. It is mammal. It live in North America, Asia, Europe. It live in desert.

Hedgehog eat insects, snails, snakes, bird eggs and grass. It is omnivore. It is nocturnal because it eat food at night.

Something unusual about my animal is that spines come out when hedgehog is scared. It roll into a ball. It has enemies like owl, fox, mongoose and wolf.

Ms. Meldonian commented on the draft as follows: "Joseph, check the *s* at the end of third-person verbs."

Phase 3: Editing

Many teachers may ask their students to self-edit because they believe that students should be given the opportunity to self-correct their work. However, students who are in the first three stages of English language acquisition will not be able to self-edit, as they will have trouble finding most of their mistakes and may be frustrated in the attempt.

Regularly conferencing with each ELL to discuss his or her works in progress is an excellent strategy for building writing skills. This is particularly true for students at the early stages of acquisition, as peer editing is not possible for them and may in fact be counterproductive. When students are fluent enough to discuss their written ideas and thoughts, the teacher should provide instruction on how to peer edit using think-alouds and modeling. For example, Ms. Meldonian had Joseph work with a partner to check the *s* at the end of third-person verbs.

Phase 4: Revising

It is important to tie the type of revision that is possible for each learner to his or her stage of language acquisition. For example, students in the early stages may not yet have developed the skills for describing possessives and tenses; they may only just be learning how to write nouns in the plural form and match them to the correct verb forms. When reviewing students' papers, teachers need to provide ELLs with specific details about what they are supposed to do during the revision process. Simply stating, "Add more information here" is too vague; a more appropriate comment would be "Mention something special that hedgehogs can do here." If students are a part of the editing process, the revisions will be more meaningful to them.

Presenting a Finished Document

Teachers should encourage students to share their writing with classmates and family. Students can display work in the classroom and hallway or "publish" classroom books. The groups in Joseph's class designed habitats for their animals, which they drew on posters and displayed in the hallway.

In this chapter, we examined the writing needs of ELLs and Calkins's four-stage writing process. Writing is an essential component of learning English and requires instruction that is matched to each student stage of English language acquisition. Homework and assessment must also be targeted to the English learning levels of students. In the next chapter, we will discuss how to provide ELLs with appropriate homework assignments and how to assess their content learning.

CHAPTER SEVEN

Homework and Assessment for ELLs

One of the students in Mrs. McBride's 6th grade ESL class, Yeon Jae, rested his head on the table. He closed his eyes and nearly fell asleep. He had appeared tired and inattentive during the class period.

Mrs. McBride asked, "Yeon Jae, are you sick?"

"I don't go sleep until 2:00 a.m.," moaned Yeon Jae. "I do work to finish homework for Mr. Fielding."

When Mrs. McBride questioned him further, she found that he had begun his homework at 5:00 p.m.—meaning he had spent nine hours on one night's assignments. Yeon Jae assumed that he was required to complete the assignments written on the board in his classroom. Mrs. McBride reviewed his homework planner (Figure 7.1).

When questioning Mr. Fielding about the homework assignments, Mrs. McBride found that he knew Yeon Jae would not be able to complete the same homework assignments as the rest of the class and just assumed that his ELLs would do the best that they could. It didn't occur to him to modify the homework, and he was dismayed to learn how late Yeon Jae had worked.

*   *   *

Figure 7.1
Yeon Jae's Homework Planner

12/7/08	
Math	Do problems 1–10 on page 50.
Social studies	Read pages 71–82 on the causes of the Civil War and answer questions 1, 2, and 3 at the end of the chapter.
English	Read the sentences on page 56 of your English book. For each sentence, underline the subject phrase with one line and verb phrase with double line.
Science	Read pages 56–74 on reflection and answer questions 1 and 2 on page 74.

Assigning homework to and assessing ELLs are often viewed as a dilemma by teachers. Some teachers, like Mr. Fielding, do not think about the difficulty that students like Yeon Jae will have with homework assignments or assessments intended for English-fluent students. These teachers leave it to the students to do what they can. Other teachers do not assign homework, tests, or quizzes to their ELLs. Still others believe that ELLs should not be treated any differently from their peers and should complete the same assignments and take the same tests. None of these responses effectively address the challenge of assigning homework to and assessing ELLs.

When considering appropriate homework and assessment for ELLs, teachers need to first determine the English proficiency levels of their ELLs. The teacher's goal should be to make learning accessible and meaningful for every student without lowering expectations or sacrificing rigor. Then, teachers must consider the overarching unit objectives and the day's content objective and assign homework that is directly related to both.

Viewing Homework and Assessment as the Continuation of a Lesson

Teachers usually assign homework to extend the time that students have to learn content and apply new knowledge. To help students master new skills, it is important to furnish them with practice and application opportunities that are not too far beyond their abilities or respective stages of English proficiency. Mr. Fielding assigned homework without modeling it or providing his students with practice time. He also did not take into account his ELLs' stages of English language acquisition.

Using language to learn content is at the core of appropriate homework assignments. Because most homework assignments require students to read and write, they present a unique challenge to ELLs. For example, students in Mr. Fielding's class were required to answer questions in their social studies textbook. However, he had not taken time to preteach the concepts, vocabulary, or types of questions that were included in the chapter, assuming instead that his students would learn what they needed to as they read the chapter. He did not modify the homework assignment for Yeon Jae, who was at the emerging stage of language acquisition and therefore not yet capable of independently reading text without the necessary prereading activities. Explicit instruction on how to complete the homework was sorely lacking in Mr. Fielding's class. Teachers must select homework assignments that are suitable for ELLs to complete independently, but without lowering the expectation that all students can learn the content objectives.

To begin the process of determining appropriate homework assignments, it is helpful to think backward about the steps necessary for homework to be accomplished. We believe that homework should be the last of the following five steps:

1. Introducing the day's lesson by reviewing the unit's overarching objectives and the day's content and language objectives
2. Modeling the day's activities
3. Having students engage in the same types of activities that they will do as homework
4. Reviewing the day's content and language objectives to determine if they have been accomplished
5. Assigning homework

Teachers typically provide lessons within the context of a thematic unit of study. Daily lessons are intended to help students achieve overarching objectives. The first step of the day's lesson should be to focus student attention on the day's language and content objectives and how they relate to the unit objectives. When these three objectives are made explicit, ELLs can more readily focus on them. It is a good idea to post the three objectives along with key vocabulary on the board.

Teachers should open their lessons by reviewing the unit objectives and the lesson's content objectives with students. It is important to revisit the unit goals often and link them explicitly to all lessons. Mr. Fielding might have posted the overarching objective for his students in the form of the following question: "How do differences between people lead to conflict?" The day's content objective might have been formulated as a question as well: "What were the five key causes of the Civil War?" Because Mr. Fielding expected his students to read a chapter in their textbooks about the five main causes of the Civil War, he might have discussed one of the causes with his students so that they had an idea of what to look for in the text.

Next, teachers should review the language objectives for the day. When considering language objectives, teachers must keep homework assignments in mind. For example, if students are to solve a word problem as homework, the teacher must first review the vocabulary that is used in the problem, how the vocabulary and word problem relate to the unit objectives, and what the process of solving a word problem entails.

As we noted earlier in this book, it is also very important to review assignments and ensure that they are connected to students' background knowledge and are not culturally biased. For example, many ELLs are not familiar with any U.S. history, so the content and vocabulary must be carefully taught to ensure understanding. Teachers must also be proactive about including explanations and illustrations of key content vocabulary. Among the terms that Mr. Fielding might explain for his lesson are *abolitionist, nonabolitionist, states' rights,* and *federal rights.*

Modeling

Next, the teacher should model the day's activities and share how they relate to the overarching unit objective. The teacher should conduct think-alouds about the steps needed to complete all tasks, including those assigned for homework, and model the tasks as well. Prior to the lesson, the teacher will need to gather the materials necessary for modeling and for student practice of the tasks. Modeling is an opportune moment to use authentic materials. Teachers should narrate their modeling with thoughts about the task.

Here is a think-aloud that Mr. Fielding might have conducted, modeling how to determine one of the causes of the Civil War:

> If I look at our chapter, there is a bulleted phrase that says: abolitionist versus nonabolitionist. I have to think about what each term means. I ask myself, "An abolitionist—what is that?" I know that an abolitionist was someone who believed that slavery should end. So, a *non*abolitionist must be someone who believed that slavery should continue.
>
> I know that there were people who didn't believe in slavery, the abolitionists, and I know that there were people who did, the nonabolitionists. When I consider our overarching question—How do differences between people lead to conflict?— I can see that the struggle between abolitionists and nonabolitionists was one of the five major causes of the Civil War.

Reviewing Objectives and Assigning Homework

Teachers should be sure to give students multiple opportunities to use content language during practice work. One way to do this is by planning different types of practice work according to the sequence shown in Figure 7.2. At the same time, it is import to continually remind students of the overarching unit

Figure 7.2
Recommended Sequence of Lesson Practice Work

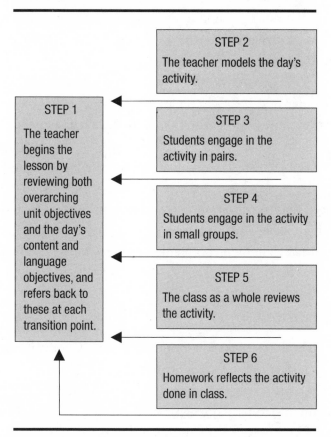

objectives and the lesson's content objectives and language objectives (by reviewing the objectives at the start of each new activity, for example). The arrows in Figure 7.2 reflect transition points in a lesson—at each transition, the teacher refers back to the unit and lesson objectives.

Teachers should take the time during the many transitions in a day's lesson to focus student attention on unit and lesson objectives and to point out the relation between classroom activities and the day's homework assignment. When assigning homework, teachers should ensure that ELLs can complete it in a reasonable amount of time. A short but meaningful homework assignment will yield better results than a long confusing one.

For homework, Mr. Fielding asked his students to answer the questions at the end of the chapter that they had just read. He might have better prepared his students for this assignment by engaging them in a discussion about the type of questions that they were to answer. Had he done this, he would have noticed that the questions were all comprehension based, and he might have had his students work in pairs to create and respond to their own comprehension questions.

Assessment

Most school districts draw from local, state, or federal curriculum standards to set student performance goals and benchmarks. High-stakes testing is used to measure how well the curriculum standards are being met and to determine whether or not a school is succeeding. Such tests often do not take into account the particular needs of ELLs. For this reason, we do not believe that high-stakes tests designed for English-fluent students should be regarded as an accurate measure of ELL ability. To ensure that tests do reflect the learning of ELLs, we suggest that teachers take the following steps:

1. Identify the English proficiency levels of their students.
2. Review the curriculum standards that they will use to create content and language objectives.

3. Select performance indicators that are appropriate for students' English proficiency levels.
4. Design rubrics that reflect students' English proficiency levels.
5. Share and provide direct instruction about the rubrics with students.

We separate assessment into three different types:

- In-the-moment assessments, which occur as the teachers observe students engaging in classroom activities;
- Routine assessments, such as teacher evaluation of quizzes, journal entries, and homework; and
- Summative assessments, such as teacher evaluation of student work at the end of a unit (i.e., final presentations, tests, theme projects).

Guidelines for Different Stages of English Language Acquisition

Here are some guidelines for assessing students at different stages of English language acquisition:

Stage 1 (Starting) and Stage 2 (Emerging)

- Ask questions that require one- or two-word responses.
- Have students point to or circle the correct picture in response to questions.
- Have students illustrate a sequence (e.g., the steps of a science experiment, or how a caterpillar becomes a butterfly) to demonstrate understanding.
- Provide a word bank so that students do not have to generate English vocabulary themselves. Students can

then label diagrams or fill in charts using words from the word bank.

- Use visuals or realia to elicit information (e.g., the pictures of volcanoes in Mrs. Mahoney's class).
- Allow students to use drawings, dioramas, graphs, maps, and charts to demonstrate comprehension.
- Allow students to gesture or act out responses.
- Provide cloze activities using sentences straight from the text.
- Use portfolio assessment for writing.
- Keep a file of student writing in order to measure growth.
- Audiotape the oral output of ELLs on a regular basis so that progress may be noted.

Stage 3 (Developing) and Stage 4 (Expanding)

- Give short tests frequently rather than long tests infrequently.
- Base assessments on the previous night's homework assignment.
- Use graphic organizers. For example, a KWL chart can show what students have learned. Brainstorm the "What I Know" part of the chart with the whole class. At the end of the unit, have ELLs complete the "What I Learned" part by drawing pictures and labeling them. You can also use a graphic organizer with information already filled in: Review the information in class, have students study it at home before the assessment, and then delete key words or phrases from the organizer to test comprehension.

- Have students role-play to show understanding of a topic. Group ELLs with English-fluent students so that they have support for their language use.
- In place of writing a report, have students show comprehension by designing a poster, diorama, bookmark, or book cover.
- Provide simplified study guides and limit assessment to items on the guide. Only key vocabulary and concepts should be covered.
- Allow students to answer essay questions orally.
- Have students compare and contrast concepts previously taught in class.
- Reformat the test so that the type is larger and there is more white space.
- Use a dialogue journal to discuss specific topics with students. English language learners respond to a particular question in the journal, and the teacher comments on the response in an ongoing discussion.
- Simplify the language of essay questions or break them into manageable parts. Read questions aloud, modifying the language as you do so.
- Limit multiple-choice questions to two possible answers.
- Tell ELLs in advance exactly what they are required to study for a test.
- Allow more time for ELLs to take a test, or ask them fewer questions.
- Highlight key words or clues on tests for ELLs. (This works especially well for math.)
- Scaffold student responses to essay questions through discussion, brainstorming, and webbing. Allow students

to use a translation dictionary or electronic translator when writing essays.

Stage 5 (Bridging)

- Identify student gaps in listening, speaking, reading, and writing, and deliver lessons that are specifically geared toward closing the gaps.
- Identify how students should show understanding of subject matter through listening, speaking, reading, and writing.
- Continue to support student writing and vocabulary development.

Assessment Rubrics

Teachers should create assessment rubrics by selecting no more than two or three of the bulleted suggestions for each stage of English proficiency noted above. For example, to assess students at the starting and emerging stages of English language acquisition, a teacher might require them to respond to "what" and "where" questions with one- or two-word responses or through gestures. For the same lesson, students at the developing and expanding stages might be required to retell or recount a story. Teachers can use the assessment rubrics to conduct in-the-moment assessments as students engage in classwork. These rubrics can help teachers to determine what adjustments they might need to make to lessons as they are occurring. Teachers should share these rubrics with students and model what in-the-moment assessment will look like. Monitoring charts are useful for this purpose. For example, Mrs. Kim used a monitoring chart to observe four ELLs in her science class as they engaged in small-group tasks (see Figure 7.3). She created the monitoring chart based on the students' stages of English language acquisition. For each student, she wrote down the stage he or she was in, the tasks that she expected to observe, and whether or not she observed the student engaging in the task. She referred to the chart while monitoring the students' interactions, marking it with a check each time she observed a student engaging in the expected tasks.

Figure 7.3
Mrs. Kim's Monitoring Chart

Students	Expected Task	Task Observed	Task Not Observed
Claudia (Stage 1 – Starting)	Pointing to correct sequence in scientific method	✔✔✔ ✔	
Stephan (Stage 2 – Emerging)	Using short phrases to describe steps of the scientific method		✔
Yosef (Stage 3 – Developing)	Using a graphic organizer to explain the scientific method	✔	
Eduardo (Stage 4 – Expanding)	Describing the steps of the scientific method using sentences		
Hoa Lia (Stage 5 – Bridging)	Synthesizing information about the scientific method	✔	

Once teachers have modeled the monitoring process, they can conduct in-the-moment checks for understanding by circulating the classroom, carefully observing student interactions, and providing additional modeling, clarifying, and direct instruction for individual and small groups of students. In addition, students should be asked to assess their own classwork periodically using a rubric such as the one shown in Figure 7.4.

Memorization

Many ELLs manage to get by in school by memorizing material, especially for quizzes and tests. But memorizing material is by no means the same as understanding it. Yeon Jae was able to get ahead by memorizing large chunks of material because Mr. Fielding's tests were taken directly from a study guide designed for native English speakers. A few weeks after Yeon Jae received a *B* on a test about the U.S. government, Judie asked him what the House of Representatives was. It was obvious to her that Yeon Jae did not retain the information that he had memorized.

Teachers should modify assessments so that ELLs are not encouraged to memorize and regurgitate material that they really don't understand. Assessment of ELLs should focus on the students' growth rather than on comparisons to their English-fluent classmates. Assessments should increasingly become more challenging as students acquire a higher proficiency level in English.

*   *   *

Figure 7.4
Sample Student Self-Assessment Rubric

Student Name: _____ **Date:** _____

Subject: _____ **Topic:** _____

Paired Work	I did not understand.	I asked questions.	I shared a few ideas. I understand some of the content and how to talk about it.	I contributed many ideas because I understand most of the content and can talk using it.
Group Work	I did not understand.	I asked questions.	I shared a few ideas. I understand some of the content and how to talk about it.	I contributed many ideas with my group because I understand most of the content.
Whole-Class Work	I did not understand.	I asked questions.	I shared a few ideas. I understand some of the content and how to talk about it.	I contributed many ideas with the whole class because I understand most of the content.

After learning about Yeon Jae's difficulties with homework, Mr. Fielding took the time to learn about his level of English language acquisition and determined his limitations. During class, he provided a handout to students explaining new vocabulary. He had each student write a definition of a term and illustrate it. Knowing that Yeon Jae was at the emerging stage of English language acquisition, he asked him to draw additional pictures illustrating new terms for homework and told him to spend no more than 45 minutes on the assignment. When Yeon Jae began the assignment, he felt confident that he could complete it—and after 45 minutes, he almost had.

In this chapter, we discussed techniques for assigning homework and creating assessments that are appropriate for the stages of English language acquisition of the ELLs in your class. In the next chapter, we will look at ways to conference with the parents of ELLs and include them in their children's education.

CHAPTER EIGHT

Communicating Effectively with Parents of ELLs

8

Ms. Ramon, a 3rd grade teacher, was concerned about the progress of one of her ELLs, Yuki, so she held a conference with Yuki's parents in October. Yuki had moved to the United States from Japan 18 months ago, and although she was able to complete some of her science and social studies work, she was not making the progress that Ms. Ramon expected.

Ms. Ramon explained to Yuki's parents that the girl needed to spend more time completing homework and studying for tests. She outlined a homework plan and asked the parents to help her implement it. The parents nodded in apparent agreement.

In the weeks after the conference, Yuki's efforts did not improve, and Ms. Ramon was at a loss to understand why. She was unaware of some important cultural considerations. In many Asian countries, to nod in agreement means, "Yes, I hear you," not, "Yes, I agree." Ms. Ramon was also unaware that Yuki spent a few hours each day completing homework from her Japanese Saturday school. Yuki's mother was very concerned that if her daughter didn't keep up with her Japanese studies, she would be at a great disadvantage when she ever returned to Japan, as she was expected to do.

*   *   *

Parent–teacher conferences are shaped by the beliefs and background knowledge of their participants. Many parents of ELLs are not familiar with the practice of meeting with their children's teachers and thus are not sure what to expect of them during the meetings. Similarly, many classroom teachers have never communicated with parents who do not speak English and who are not familiar with U.S. public school practices. The increasing population of ELLs poses a unique challenge for classroom teachers, administrators, and guidance counselors, all of whom need to learn how to better communicate with linguistically and culturally diverse families. The goal of this chapter is to help school personnel hold productive parent–teacher conferences by engaging in meaningful communication.

Translators

The first step in planning a conference with the parents of ELLs is to determine whether a translator is needed, as many parents do not speak English well enough to understand what the teacher is saying. It is crucial to the success of a conference to contact a translator for the parents who need one. Most parents are asked to complete a Home Language Survey (see Appendix 3) when they enroll their child in school. On this survey, parents should be asked for the language in which they would prefer oral and written communication from the school. Although the survey is crucial, it should not be the only means used to determine whether or not families need a translator; because some parents may not understand what they are being asked and others may not feel comfortable letting the school know that they are not fluent in English, a high level of sensitivity is needed to complete this task well. A parent once told Judie that when she first came to the United States, she faked her way through her child's conferences without understanding a word. If your school does not provide translators, ask parents to bring a bilingual family member along to the meetings (not counting the actual student). It is best to meet with translators before the conference to ensure that they understand the purpose of the occasion.

When a translator is used, we suggest doubling the length of the conference to account for the extra time required for translation. During the conference, teachers should speak in short, uncomplicated sentences and stop periodically to let the translator translate. If a teacher goes on too long without stopping, his or her whole message may not be accurately translated. Teachers should refrain from using educational jargon, as neither the translator nor the parents are likely to understand it, and should avoid speaking directly to the translator. We have been present at conferences were parents felt so superfluous that they took phone calls right in the middle of the conversation while the teacher and translator spoke with each other.

Welcoming Parents

Schools often find it challenging to engage parents in attending school functions, including conferences. Parents may not attend because they do not have transportation or may feel embarrassed by their lack of English or literacy skills. They may also come from cultures where parents are not welcomed into the school. To address such obstacles, teachers must believe in the importance of becoming familiar with students' families and think of ways to involve them in their students' education in a welcoming and nonthreatening manner. Schools need to consider that parents may not be able to read the notices that come home, even those that have been translated. An oral invitation issued in the parents' native language may be helpful. Arranging for transportation and child care as well as translation services may also encourage parents to come to school.

Guidelines for Preconference Planning

Here are some guidelines for planning a successful conference:

- Prepare a short, simply worded description of the conference that includes the date, location, anticipated start and end times, and goals. Have the document translated if necessary and mail it to parents.
- Assemble samples of each student's work to share with his or her parents.
- If possible, have report cards and rubrics translated.
- Prepare an outline of the conference agenda to show to parents and make sure that it includes topics that they will want to discuss.
- Try to schedule the conference so that both parents can attend. In some cultures, no important decisions are made without the father's agreement.

Teachers may also want to have visuals and manipulatives ready for use during the conference, particularly if no translator will be present. Judie once sat in a conference with a kindergarten teacher who illustrated a student's issues with math by using the math manipulatives from her classroom to explain what the child was able to do and what he needed to work on.

Greeting Parents

Teachers should be sure to have their body language reflect a warm and receptive attitude. They should greet parents just as they would greet guests in their homes—that is, at the door, not from across the room behind a desk.

There are diverse cultural norms about whom it is appropriate to touch in different cultures. For example, in some cultures, shaking hands is not an acceptable greeting. In many Asian cultures, a nod and slight bow are preferred; many Muslim males will not touch or shake hands with women; and people in Thailand and India often greet each other by clasping their own hands together. It is a good idea to wait and see if the parent offers his or her hand first. Even in cultures where handshaking is customary, the manner in which it is done may differ from the U.S. norm. In most of the world, a simple handclasp is considered more appropriate than the more vigorous, hand-pumping style common in the United States.

Body Language

Because the conference is serious business, the teacher's body language (including demeanor and dress) should convey as much. Teachers should sit up straight in their chairs and not fold their arms in front of them. They should also refrain from using hand gestures, as these may have unintended meanings in different cultures. Male teachers should not sit with the foot of one leg on the knee of another. Here are some additional concerns to keep in mind:

Personal space. Teachers need to consider how close they stand to people of other cultures. It is customary in the United States to stand at arm's length from others. In Asia, people stand a little farther away; in Latin America and in the Middle East, they will stand closer. A U.S. teacher's impulse might be to step back when someone stands too close, but this impulse should be controlled during conferences, lest the teacher offend students' parents. It is better instead for the teacher to take the opportunity to move toward the conferencing area.

If possible, teachers should set up the conference area with adult-size chairs. Because a direct face-to-face arrangement may come across as too confrontational or intimate for some parents, it is best to arrange chairs so that the teacher is at a 45-degree angle from the parents. If a translator is present, he or she should sit next to the parents, not the teacher.

Eye contact. In the United States, avoiding eye contact suggests untrustworthiness. In Asia, however, too much eye contact is considered rude and confrontational. It is therefore important for teachers not to take avoidance of eye contact personally and to keep eye contact intermittent. (Sitting at a 45-degree angle helps to ensure that this is done.)

Smiling. The U.S. custom of smiling when greeting someone is not universal. Teachers should smile when greeting parents and throughout the conference, but they should not become alarmed if a parent doesn't smile back. Also, teachers should keep in mind that smiles may indicate embarrassment or even anger; they should not assume that they always signify agreement.

Names

The Western custom of given names followed by surnames and of changing surnames upon marriage is not followed in some cultures. For example, many Korean and Chinese women do not take their husbands' names. A teacher may say to a mother, "You are the mother of Se Hung Lee. What name should I call you?" In general, children from Spanish-speaking families have a given name followed by two surnames: the first surname is the father's family name, and the second one is the mother's family name. It is also traditional in all Spanish-speaking countries for women to retain their family names when they get married—so the mother of Carolina Rodriguez Hernandez, for example, might be called Mrs. Hernandez, and her father, Mr. Rodriguez. In Argentina and some other South American countries, most women either take their husbands' names as they do in the United States or keep their last names but follow it with the preposition "de" and the husband's last name. In such a case, Carolina's mother would be Mrs. Hernandez de Rodriguez.

To avoid unnecessary confusion, teachers should review their students' school registration forms to see how parents sign their names. Judie once had a Japanese student who had a different family name from his parents and older brother. When she asked the parents about this, they told her that their second son was given the mother's family name because her parents only had female offspring and they didn't want the name to die out.

Low-Context and High-Context Cultures

Cultures such as the United States, where verbal communication is usually direct and there is little need for nonverbal cues in order for people to understand each other, are considered low-context cultures. Other characteristics of low-context cultures include favoring individual rights over duty to one's family and not taking umbrage at simple differing viewpoints. High-context cultures, by contrast, generally place greater value on group harmony and family loyalty. They are also very often hierarchical and traditional and give much more importance to such concepts as shame and honor than low-context cultures do. In high-context cultures, words tend to be chosen more carefully, as are expressions conveying respect and courtesy.

Most U.S. immigrants come from high-context cultures such as Latin America, Asia, and the Middle East. Parents from such cultures may be silent when considering responses to teacher questions, and they may also avoid expressing disagreement out of a fear of disharmony. We know of many incidences where parents have moved rather than express their disagreement with a school! Too often, U.S. educators feel that they have reached an agreement simply because parents have not voiced disagreement.

We have noticed that teachers use a lot of circuitous language when bringing a student problem to attention. Although English-fluent parents are able to read between the lines in these situations, the parents of ELLs often are not. For this reason, it is best to be as clear and direct as possible.

Let's look at an example of miscommunication between a family from a high-context culture and the educators at a U.S. school. Amal, a 6th grade boy from Egypt, is frequently in trouble because he constantly touches other boys on the playground and hallways of the school. He never hurts anyone, but his classmates are uncomfortable with his behavior and begin to taunt and bully him. His father is called into the school for a conference but doesn't understand why the principal and teacher are upset.

Amal doesn't change his behavior. One day his classmates gang up on him after school and beat him up. Amal's enraged father returns to the school this time with an adult nephew who had gone to high school in the United States. The nephew immediately knows what the problem is and tells his uncle that in the United States, boys do not touch each other very much unless they are involved in sports or are fighting—unlike in Egypt, where boys constantly touch each other while playing.

The students who ganged up on Amal are punished. After the meeting, Amal learns to keep his hands to himself and begins to make some friends. From this incident, the school learns that it is important to make an effort to understand the cultures of their students and their families.

Let's consider another example. Mrs. Miller is an exemplary 4th grade teacher who excels at conferencing with the parents of her ELLs. She requests a conference with the parents of one of her ELLs, Marguerite Castellanos, because she is concerned that Marguerite is having trouble with science and social studies and does not complete her homework. Before the conference,

Mrs. Miller checks the school records and finds that Marguerite's parents both use the surname Castellanos.

At the beginning of the conference, Mrs. Miller greets Marguerite's parents and their translator, Nita, at the door of her classroom. She invites them to sit at a table in the back of the room, where she has assembled all of Marguerite's work samples. She has an agenda for the meeting that she shares with Mr. and Mrs. Castellanos and Nita. Mrs. Miller speaks in short sentences and enunciates her words clearly. She is careful to speak directly to the parents rather than Nita, and she stops frequently so that Nita can translate what she has said.

Mrs. Miller begins by showing the parents evidence of Marguerite's strengths using samples of her best work. She praises Marguerite's grasp of spoken English and explains how she sometimes translates for other children. She then demonstrates to parents the areas on which she wants to focus with Marguerite during the upcoming weeks. She shows the parents examples of the types of activities that Marguerite will be engaging in and the vocabulary that she will need to learn. She shows them an example of the upcoming test and of homework assignments. She states her expectations clearly and explicitly, not expecting the parents to read between the lines, but also tactfully, so that the parents don't feel as if they're losing face. She doesn't say that Marguerite is not doing well in science or social studies but, rather, explains her expectations for 4th graders and invites the parents to suggest ways to help Marguerite succeed. She focuses on what can be done in the future instead of placing blame for what has not been done in the past. She discusses the importance of homework and how long it should take.

Mrs. Miller ends the conference on a positive note by sharing a story about how kind Marguerite was to a new student. She gives the parents a piece of paper enumerating the main points that she made during the meeting, so that they can review the information with the translator. After the conference, whenever Marguerite shows progress, Mrs. Miller writes her parents celebratory letters. (Although some teachers will routinely telephone parents, Mrs. Miller realizes that Mr. and Mrs. Castellanos do not have a sufficient command of English to hold a meaningful conversation on the phone.)

Differing Views on Time

In the United States, Canada, and Northern European countries, time is expected to be highly structured, efficiency is revered, and people generally focus on one event or interaction at a time. These countries are monochronic. By contrast, the countries of Latin America, the Caribbean, the Middle East, Southern Europe, and Africa are by and large polychronic: Time is less structured, and people may more readily attend to many things at once, hold several conversations at the same time, or talk over each other in conversation.

In monochronic countries such as the United States, punctuality is valued and tardiness is considered disrespectful. In polychronic countries, however, appointment times and deadlines are seen more as approximations, so tardiness is not considered that big a deal. This difference in attitude toward time poses a problem for schools that have a conference schedule to meet. One school that we know changed the wording on the conference reminder so that it included an end time as well as a beginning time ("Your conference will begin at 2:30 p.m. and will finish at 3:15 p.m."). Teachers in this school are encouraged to keep their appointments on time so that parents who leave work or hire babysitters are not kept waiting. Another school has a bilingual staff member write a letter in Spanish to explain how the conferences are scheduled and how important it is to be at school on time. One teacher told us that she schedules a chronically late parent for the last appointment of the day.

Teachers often tell us that their students from polychronic cultures are often late or miss school. We believe that strong, continuous communication with parents will help administrators and teachers address these cultural differences. In many cultures, family unity is the most important value. Children will miss school, often without warning, for a myriad of family reasons. One 11-year-old student we know of—a boy named Miguel, who was originally from Mexico—missed 13 days of school because his grandmother was hospitalized and he was responsible for translating for his family when they talked to doctors and nurses. He was the oldest English-speaking member of his family. Miguel's parents never notified the school to explain why he would be absent, so he was declared truant. If the parents and teachers at Miguel's school had been communicating on a regular basis, Miguel's parents would have been more likely to explain his absences, and he would have been able to make up for the worked he missed. As a truant, however, he received a failing grade for the work.

Building Relationships That Extend Beyond Parent Conferences

According to research by Scribner, Young, and Pedroza (1999), when parents are actively involved in the education of their children, the children are more likely to do better in school, attend school regularly, graduate, and go on to college. For this reason, school administrators and teachers need to take the initiative in establishing meaningful communications with parents from diverse cultures.

Effective parent communication involves building relationships with parents and families that extend beyond parent–teacher conferences and are directly linked to what is occurring in the classroom and school. We believe that teachers should actively seek ways to connect the curriculum to students' families so that parents and other caregivers can be active partners in their children's education.

There are many ways for parents of ELLs to be engaged, regardless of their levels of literacy, prior schooling, or fluency in English. First, teachers should create lessons that require students to routinely gather information from their families, perhaps by interviewing them or by inviting family members to visit the class. Bloom, Katz, Solsken, Willett, and Wilson Keenan (2000) note that parental visits to the classroom can prove beneficial to students. Envisioning the parents of ELLs as assets or partners with something important to offer can prove very helpful. For example, Debbie worked in a district that provided an after-school Spanish enrichment program in one of its elementary schools. The purpose of the program was to foster more bilingualism and cross-cultural awareness among

English-fluent students and ELLs. The students in the program wrote a play entirely in Spanish and performed it before, during, and after school. The ELLs enlisted their mothers, some of whom were seamstresses, to make the play's costumes. Each of the performances had a fully packed auditorium of parents, including all of the parents of the ELLs in the district, many of whom had never come to their children's school.

Teachers, administrators, and other stakeholders must take time to welcome and encourage parent involvement in ways that are respectful, honoring, and valuing. This includes taking the steps needed to employ translators, prepare for meetings, design and implement activities for involving parents, and encourage parent involvement. When this is done well, teachers and parents become active partners in their children's education. In our next chapter, we will demonstrate how the strategies from this book can be applied to a math lesson.

CHAPTER NINE

Effective ELL
Instruction in Action

9

M s. Frechette was teaching a middle school math unit on similarity. She knew that her ELLs were at different stages of English language acquisition and that she needed to provide them with in-class practice geared to their levels of English proficiency. She also knew that she had to provide her ELLs with step-by-step instructions for homework assignments that explicitly connected the assignments to her overarching objective (that students will understand the concept of similarity). Ms. Frechette had taken time to learn about the English proficiency levels of her ELLs and had created the day's lesson with them in mind. Let's look closely at two of the ELLs in Ms. Frechette's class and the ways in which she addressed their respective proficiency levels.

Maria had been in the United States for six months. She was in Stage 2 (emerging) of English language acquisition, so she was building understanding of vocabulary and content through a good deal of visual support. She was able to provide one-word responses to questions and could participate actively when Ms. Frechette used body language and illustrations to describe the activities that were required of her. She also relied heavily on the information that Ms. Frechette displayed on the board and in the class handouts. Ms. Frechette usually called on Maria when she expected a yes/no, either/or, or same/different response. Maria's strength was in naming key vocabulary words and writing very simple sentences to go with the key words.

Li arrived from Beijing 15 months ago. She was in Stage 3 (developing) of English language acquisition, so she understood and could work with modified content that allowed her to make connections with background knowledge and provide brief descriptions and summaries of content material.

At the beginning of class, Ms. Frechette shared her objectives for the lesson with students by posting them on the board and passing them out in a handout (see Figure 9.1). (The objectives would remain on the board for the duration of the two-week unit.) She read the overarching unit objective aloud, followed by the day's content and language objectives, and told her students that they would be learning about ratios to describe similarities. She wrote the word *similarity* on the board.

Next, Ms. Frechette divided her class into pairs, assigning Maria and Li to partners whom she believed would support them. She asked each pair to discuss the meaning of the word *similarity* and then to share its ideas with another pair. Once this task was completed, she asked each pair to agree on a definition that it believed best describes the word. Each pair shared its definition with the whole class, after which Ms. Frechette asked the class as a whole to agree on a single definition. Each student voted for one of the definitions. The definition with the most votes was as follows: "*Similarity* refers to the ways in which people, places, and things are the same." Ms. Frechette asked the students to write the chosen definition next to the word *similarity* on their handouts and to draw a picture illustrating the term. She then conducted a think-aloud as to what her own drawing might look like and drew it on the board.

Figure 9.1
Ms. Frechette's Handout

Unit Objective	To understand how to describe things that are similar mathematically
Content Objectives	1. Listen to a definition about ratios. 2. Write a ratio as a fraction. 3. Solve ratio problems using fractions. 4. Prepare for homework assignment about ratios.
Language Objective	To learn to compare the relationship between two quantities using ratios

Word	Definition	Example
Similarity		
Ratio		
Quantities		
Fractional Ratios		

Activity: With a partner, describe a quantity that can be measured using a fractional ratio and percentage.

Part	Total	Fractional Ratio	Percentage
7 girls	Out of 25 students	7/25	27%

Ms. Frechette told her students that they would be learning about ratios to describe the relationship between similar people, places, or things. On the board, above the word *similarity*, she wrote, "Vocabulary words about ratios." Beneath *similarity*, she wrote, "*ratio* = comparing two or more quantities." She then explained that quantities could be either numbers or measurements. Beneath the definition of *ratio*, she wrote, "*quantity* = numbers or measurement." She then explained that a fraction is used to compare the part-to-whole relationship of a quantity. Beneath the definition of *quantity*, she wrote, "the ratio of girls in our class." As she wrote this, Maria's partner shared the meaning of these words with Maria by pointing to the girls in their class. Maria nodded to her partner, indicating that she understood. Before moving on, Ms. Frechette revisited the overarching unit objective and discussed it with the class.

Next, Ms. Frechette conducted another think-aloud. She noted that in order to determine the ratio of girls in the class, she must first find out the total number of students. She counted aloud and stated that there were 25 students in the class. She wrote this number on the board. Then, she counted the number of girls in the room and wrote the number 7 above the number 25 on the board, placing a line between the two numbers. She told the students that the ratio of girls in the class could be described as a fraction: 7/25. "There are 25 students," she said. "For me to describe a fraction of the students, I have to write a ratio statement. My ratio statement is that 7/25ths of the students in our class are girls."

Ms. Frechette asked each pair of students to discuss different ideas that they had for measuring ratios of similar people, places, or things in their classroom. She told them to select something from the classroom to measure. On the board, she used the same chart as in the activity section of her handout to spark students' thinking about comparing. Under the word "part," she wrote "7 girls," and under the word "total," she wrote, "out of 25 students." Ms. Frechette moved to where Maria and her partner were seated and listened to their discussion. Maria's partner pointed to her eyes and commented that their eye color was different. On a piece of paper, Maria's partner wrote, "Maria's eyes are blue, mine are brown." She then wrote the number 2 and handed her pencil to Maria. Maria wrote the number 1 above the number 2, placing a line between the two numbers to form a fraction, next to which she wrote the fraction again. Nodding her approval of their work, Ms. Frechette asked Maria and her partner to find something else in the room that could be compared through measurement. Maria noticed that some students had brown hair and some had blond hair. She said "brown hair and yellow hair" to her partner. On their handouts, they wrote "10 yellow hair" under "part" and "out of 25 students" under "total." Ms. Frechette affirmed their actions by saying, "Good, note the difference on your chart, and we will use this to form a fractional ratio."

Ms. Frechette then moved to the other pairs in the classroom and responded to their ideas. She then asked each pair to work with another pair to discuss the ideas that they had generated for this task. She watched Li and her partner share their ideas. Li rapidly engaged her classmates in a discussion of the types of fractional ratio measurements that she and her partner had made. She also observed as Maria and her partner engaged with another pair in the same task. She listened carefully to Maria and noticed that she used simple phrases to describe what they had chosen for their ratio example. Drawing from the various examples that the pairs had created, Ms. Frechette next asked each pair to create a descriptive statement using the following frame:

(Number) out of a total of (number and noun) in our class = (ratio). This represents (percentage) of the total.

Next, Ms. Frechette reviewed the content objectives for the lesson with her students and asked if they thought they had achieved it. All nodded in agreement, including Maria and Li. Once this was done, Ms. Frechette asked her students to review the homework assignment with her. She read the assignment aloud as she wrote it on the board: "Measure the number of similar people, places, or things in your home using ratios. Discuss this assignment with your family and ask them for help finding items to measure." She told the students to come up with four examples and to use the handout they used earlier in class to form their answers.

When Maria arrived home, she decided to tackle her math homework. After explaining the assignment to her mother, the two of them found many objects in their home that Maria could measure using fractional ratios. Using the handout from Ms. Frechette and the notes that she copied from the board during class, she identified four examples of ratios. She wrote the examples down and illustrated them. She believed that she understood the process of determining fractional ratios because Ms. Frechette had provided so many examples in class.

At the end of the week, Ms. Frechette had her students take an exam that required them to answer questions using the same type of language they used in their class activities and homework assignments. We believe that test-taking skills can and should be taught while teaching content. For example, rather than simply describing to students what an open-ended question is, teachers should have them conduct a content-based task that requires them to answer an open-ended question, and they should provide students with step-by-step instruction in doing so.

*   *   *

Here are some ways in which Ms. Frechette ensured that her lesson would be successful for the ELLs in her class:

- She introduced the lesson by reading the unit and lesson objectives out loud, and she reviewed the objectives again during each transition point to ensure that her students were aware of the purpose behind every activity. She also posted the objectives on the board and included them in her handout. At the end of the lesson, she revisited the objectives once more.
- She wrote key vocabulary on the board and had her students explore what they mean.
- She took care to ensure that her lesson did not include examples that might reflect cultural bias.
- She modeled the day's activities and homework assignment, and she provided students with several practice opportunities using diagrams.
- She divided her class into pairs, assigning her ELLs to partners with whom she believed they would work well, and asked each pair to come up with examples of fractional ratios. She supported them in this process, providing them with the time that they needed to complete the task.

- She asked each pair to share ideas with another pair, then with the whole class—a sequence that allowed students to begin their assigned activity within the safety of a small learning community and also allowed for multiple practice opportunities.
- She drew from her students' lives to create activities with which she believed her students could relate.
- She closely observed her students during each task, assessing their progress all the while.
- She made sure to ask her ELLs questions that matched their levels of English proficiency.
- She regarded the students as rich resources for one another and provided them with ample opportunities to work together.
- She required her students to provide one another with feedback, thus allowing them to make sure that they understood the material.
- She assigned homework that related directly to the day's lesson, engaged family members, and provided students with a frame for their answers. Because the assignment required students to use the language of ratios and percentages to describe their mathematical understanding about people, places, and things that are similar, Ms. Frechette was able to immediately assess her students' understanding when she reviewed their homework.

An effective instructional environment is one in which teachers

- Identify and post the core unit and lesson objectives;
- Provide authentic and compelling tasks that connect with students' background knowledge and experiences;
- Use charts, diagrams, or graphic organizers;

- Match learning activities to students' English proficiency levels; and
- Provide multiple in-class guided practice opportunities that are similar in structure to the homework assignment.

The ways in which we design and deliver instruction and organize our classrooms must continuously be focused on supporting students to be active learners in and engaged members of the school community.

APPENDIX ONE

Suggested Verbs to Use When Composing Language Objectives

Listening	Speaking
• Listen for	• Retell
• Look for	• Summarize
• Pay attention to	• Discuss
• Think about	• Share
• Focus on	• Tell
• Concentrate on	• Persuade
	• Argue
	• Report
	• Recite
	• Describe
	• Comment
	• Explain
	• Sing
	• Echo
	• Repeat
	• Read aloud
	• Present
	• Talk
	• Say
	• Whisper
	• Chant
	• Announce
	• Ask
	• Answer

Reading	Writing
• Sort	• Write
• Read	• Draw
• Find	• Copy
• Look for	• Compare
• Predict	• Contrast
• Confirm	• Draft
• Infer	• Type
• Sequence	• Label
• Identify	• Edit
• Match	• Sort
• Unscramble	• Summarize
• Find information about	• Print
• Review	• Fill in
• Organize	• Illustrate
	• Color
	• Record
	• Collect
	• Graph
	• Diagram
	• Create
	• Make

Lesson Modification
Worksheet

Teacher: _____ Grade Level: _____

Subject: _____ Unit or Chapter: _____

Acquisition stages of the ELLs in my class: _____

1. What are the ELL or content area standards?
2. What key concepts will students learn, and what strategies will be used to teach them?
3. What background knowledge will students need? How will it be activated?

4. List key terms, words, idioms, and phrases (TWIPs) to be pretaught. Include simple, student-friendly definitions. Identify words that are likely to be used outside class as well as academic words that are content-specific.

1.

2.

3.

4.

5.

6.

7.

8.

5. Design one or more of the following activities for TWIP instruction:
   - Matching vocabulary with definitions
   - Drawing and labeling
   - Labeling maps
   - Filling out simple charts
   - Sequencing activity
   - Group vocabulary activities and games
   - Student-generated word walls

6. Check which of the following strategies you will use in class:

- [ ] 1. Buddies
- [ ] 2. Cooperative groups
- [ ] 3. Graphs, charts, photos, drawings
- [ ] 4. Graphic organizers
- [ ] 5. Hands-on activities
- [ ] 6. Taping explanations and photocopying notes
- [ ] 7. Highlighting, sticky notes, Wikki Stix
- [ ] 8. Using body language, skits, storytelling, music, videos
- [ ] 9. Vocabulary box wherever possible

7. How will you modify text for beginning learners of English?

8. What kind of homework will you assign? How does it explicitly connect to and provide additional practice for the day's lesson?

9. How will you modify assessments for ELLs?

Home Language Survey

Dear Parent/Guardian,

In order to help your child succeed in school, we ask that you please fill out the following form for each child you are registering. Your answers will help us to provide the best possible educational program for your child.

Student Name: _____

Date of Birth: _____

Current Grade: _____

Country of Birth: _____

Date of family's most recent entry into the United States:

_____

What language did your child first understand or speak?

_____

What language do you use most often when speaking to your child at home? _____

What language does your child use most often when speaking with you at home? _____

What language does your child use most often when speaking with other family members? _____

What language does your child use most often when speaking to friends? _____

Does your child read in English? ☐ Yes ☐ No

Does your child read in a language
other than English? ☐ Yes ☐ No
If yes, what language? _____

Does your child write in English? ☐ Yes ☐ No

Does your child write in a language
other than English? ☐ Yes ☐ No
If yes, what language? _____

At what age did your child start attending school? _____

Has your child entered school every year
since that age? ☐ Yes ☐ No
If no, please explain: _____

_____

_____

_____

_____

APPENDIX FOUR

Glossary

Accommodation: Modifying spoken or written language to make it comprehensible to second-language learners

Adapted: Modified for English language learners; usually refers to materials that have simplified language without watering down the content

Background knowledge: Experience and knowledge that a student brings to classroom learning; also known as *prior knowledge*

Backward design: The process of designing lessons by first determining what students should be able to know and do at the conclusion of the lesson; also known as *thinking backward*

Basic interpersonal communication skills (BICS): The skills required for verbal face-to-face social communication

Big ideas: Core concepts in a school's curriculum

Bilingual: Having the ability to communicate in two languages

Chunk: A grouping of words that are usually used together as fixed expressions (e.g., "Hello, how are you?")

Cognitive academic language proficiency (CALP): The academic language of the content classroom, which takes 4–10 years for ELLs to acquire

Communicative competence: The ability to produce language appropriately both orally and in writing

Competencies: The least amount of language necessary to get by in social situations

Comprehensible input: Communication that is just above the learners' level of English ability

Content-based ESL instruction: The process of teaching language through content area subject matter

Content objectives: The material that teachers want their students to learn by the end of a lesson

Cooperative learning: The process of students working together in small groups

English for speakers of other languages (ESOL): A program of English language instruction for non-English speakers; also known as *English as a second language (ESL)*

Formative assessment: The process of assessing whether or not learning is occurring during the course of a lesson

Graphic organizer: A chart or table used to organize information and ideas

Language acquisition: The process of learning a language through meaningful, informal conversation

Language objectives: The language learning that teachers want their students to achieve by the end of a lesson

Learning style: The manner in which a given student learns

Mainstreaming: The practice of placing ELLs in classes designed for English-fluent speakers

Mentor texts: Texts that demonstrate different writing genres for writers, often used by teachers as examples of high-quality writing for students

Native language: The first language that a person learns; often the language that ELLs use at home; also known as *heritage language, home language,* and *primary language*

Sheltered English: The process of simplifying the language of instruction to teach content area material

Sheltered Instruction Observation Protocol (SIOP): A strategy for describing instructional practices that help teachers make content accessible to ELLs

Stopping places: Places in a text where students should stop to ask themselves questions or make predictions

Summative assessment: The process of assessing whether or not learning has occurred during a lesson or unit, such as through a quiz, test, or exam

Target language: The language that a learner is trying to acquire

Teachers of English to Speakers of Other Languages (TESOL): An international professional organization for those concerned with the teaching of English as a second or foreign language and of Standard English as a second dialect

Text-to-self connection: An association that students make between the text that they are reading and something that happened in their own lives

Text-to-text connection: An association that students make between the text that they are reading and another text that they have read

Text-to-world connection: An association that students make between the text that they are reading and something that has happened in the world

Think-aloud: The strategy of modeling problem-solving thought processes by narrating them for students

TWIPs: An acronym referring to terms, words, idioms, and phrases that reflect the key concepts and vocabulary of a lesson or unit

BIBLIOGRAPHY

Alexander, K., & Alexander, M. D. (1985). *American public school law*. St. Paul, MN: West Publishing.

August, D., & Shanahan, T. (Eds.). (2006). Executive summary. *Developing literacy in second language learners: Report of the National Literacy Panel on Language-Minority Children and Youth*. Mahwah, NJ: Lawrence Erlbaum.

Beck, I. L., McKeown, M. G., & Kucan, L. (2002). *Bringing words to life: Robust vocabulary instruction*. New York: The Guilford Press.

Blatner, W. (2006). *Teaching content for language development*. Unpublished paper. School of Education, University of Massachusetts at Amherst.

Bloom, D., Katz, L., Solsken, J., Willett, J., & Wilson Keenan, J. (2000, January/February). Interpellations of family/community and classroom literacy practices. *Journal of Educational Research, 93*(3), 155–163.

Caine, R. N., & Caine, G. (1991). *Making connections: Teaching and the human brain*. Reading, MA: Addison-Wesley.

Calderon, M. (2007). *Teaching reading to English language learners, grades 6–12.* Thousand Oaks, CA: Corwin Press.

Calkins, L. (1994). *The art of teaching writing* (new ed.). Portsmouth, NH: Heinemann.

Cohen, E. (1994). *Designing groupwork: Strategies for the heterogeneous classroom.* New York: Teachers College Press.

Collier, V. P. (1987). Age and rate of acquisition of second language for academic purposes. *TESOL Quarterly, 21,* 617–641.

Crandall, J., Jaramillo, A., Olsen, L., & Peyton, J. K. (2002). *Using cognitive strategies to develop English language and literacy.* Washington, DC: Center for Applied Linguistics.

Cummins, J. (1981). Age on arrival and immigrant second language learning in Canada: A reassessment. *Applied Linguistics, 2,* 132–149.

Cummins, J. (1984). *Bilingualism and special education: Issues in assessment and pedagogy.* Clevedon, United Kingdom: Multilingual Matters.

Diaz Rico, L., & Weed, K. (2006). *The cross-cultural language and academic development handbook: A complete K–12 reference guide* (3rd ed.). New York: Pearson.

Echevarria, J., Vogt, M. E., & Short, D. (2008). *Making content comprehensible for English language learners: The SIOP model* (3rd ed.). Boston: Allyn and Bacon.

Edwards, M. (1999). *Pa Lia's first day.* New York: Harcourt Brace & Co.

Faltis, C. (2001). *Joinfostering: Teaching and learning in multilingual classrooms* (3rd ed.). Upper Saddle River, NJ: Merrill/Prentice-Hall.

Faltis, C., & Hudelson, S. (1998). *Bilingual education in elementary and secondary school communities: Toward understanding and caring.* New York: Allyn and Bacon.

Freeman, D., & Freeman, Y. (2000). *Teaching reading in multilingual classrooms.* Portsmouth, NH: Heinemann.

Gardner, H. (1987, May). Beyond IQ: Education and human development. *Harvard Educational Review, 57*(2), 187–193.

Gardner, H. (1993). *Frames of mind and multiple intelligences: The theory in practice, 10th anniversary edition.* New York: Basic Books.

Goeke, J. (2009). *Explicit instruction: A framework for meaningful direct teaching.* New York: Pearson.

Gonzalez, J. M., & Darling-Hammond, L. (2000). *Programs that prepare teachers to work effectively with students learning English.* Washington, DC: Center for Applied Linguistics.

Green, J. (2005). *Tornadoes.* Washington, DC: National Geographic Society.

Harvey, S., & Goudvis, A. (2007). *Strategies that work: Teaching comprehension for understanding and engagement.* York, ME: Stenhouse Publishers.

Haynes, J. (2007). *Getting started with English language learners.* Alexandria, VA: ASCD.

Haynes, J. (2008, Fall). Holding effective parent conferences. *Essential Teacher, 5*(3), 6–7.

Haynes, J. (2009a, March). Teaching reading comprehension. *Essential Teacher, 6*(1), 6–7.

Haynes, J. (2009b, June). What good readers do. *Essential Teacher, 6*(2), 6–7.

Haynes, J. (2009c, September). What else good readers do. *Essential Teacher, 6*(3), 6–7.

Hill, J., & Flynn, K. (2008, Winter). Asking the right questions: Teachers' questions can build students' English language skills. *Journal of Staff Development, 29*(1), 46–52.

Hinkel, E. (2009, March 26). *How to adapt a textbook to meet students' learning goals.* Paper presented at the annual conference of Teachers of English to Speakers of Other Languages, Denver, Colorado.

Hudelson, S. (2001). Literacy development in second language children. In F. Genesee (Ed.), *Educating second language children: The whole child, the whole curriculum, the whole community* (pp. 129–158). New York: Cambridge Language Education.

Hunter, M. (1982). *Mastery teaching: Increasing instructional effectiveness in secondary schools, college and universities.* El Segundo, CA: TIP Publications.

Kagan, S. (1994). *Cooperative learning.* San Clemente, CA: Kagan Cooperative Learning.

Kagan, S., Kagan, M., & Kagan, L. (2000). *Reaching social studies standards through cooperative learning: Providing for all learners in general education classrooms.* Port Chester, NY: National Professional Resources, Inc.

Keene, E., & Zimmermann, S. (1997). *Mosaic of thought.* Portsmouth, NH: Heinemann.

Krashen, S. (1981). *Second language acquisition and second language learning.* Oxford, United Kingdom: Pergamon Press.

Krashen, S. (1982). *Principles and practice in second language acquisition.* Englewood Cliffs, NJ: Prentice-Hall.

Lappan, G., Fey, J. T., Fitzgerald, W. M., Friel, S. N., & Phillips, E. D. (2006). *Connected mathematics 2: Stretching and shrinking: Understanding similarity.* New York: Pearson.

Lawrence-Lightfoot, S. (2003). *The essential conversation: What parents and teachers can learn from each other.* New York: Ballantine Books.

Levine, E. (2007). *Henry's freedom box.* New York: Scholastic.

Luke, A. (1994). *Social construction of literacy in the classroom.* Melbourne, Australia: Macmillan.

Marzano, R., & Pickering, D. (2005). *Building academic vocabulary: Teachers' manual.* Alexandria, VA: ASCD.

Menzella, L. (2008). Making reading come alive. *Voices, 3.*

Miller, D. (2002). *Reading with meaning.* York, ME: Stenhouse Publishers.

Northeastern University Institute on Race and Justice. (2004, May 4). *Massachusetts racial and gender profiling technical report.* Retrieved August 17, 2009, from http://www.racial profilinganalysis.neu.edu/irjsite_docs/technicalreport.pdf

Putnam, J. (1997). *Cooperative learning in diverse classrooms.* Upper Saddle River, NJ: Prentice-Hall.

Radencich, M., & McKay, L. (Eds.). (1995). *Flexible grouping for literacy in the elementary grades.* Boston: Allyn and Bacon.

Rothstein-Fish, C., & Trumbull, E. (2008). *Managing diverse classrooms: How to build on students' cultural strengths.* Alexandria, VA: ASCD.

Scribner, J., Young, M., & Pedroza, A. (1999). Building collaborative relationships with parents. In P. Reyes, J. D. Scribner, & A. Paredes-Scribner (Eds.), *Lessons from high-performing Hispanic schools: Creating learning communities* (pp. 36–60). New York: Teachers College Press.

Short, D., Himmel, J., & Richards, C. (2009, March 27). *Developing science curriculum units with the SIOP model.* Paper presented at the annual conference of Teachers of English to Speakers of Other Languages, Denver, Colorado.

Sizer, T. (2004). *Horace's compromise.* Boston: Houghton Mifflin/ Harcourt.

Slavin, R. E. (1991, February). Synthesis of research on cooperative learning. *Educational Leadership, 48*(50), 71–82.

Slavin, R. E. (1995). *Cooperative learning: Theory, research, and practice* (2nd ed.). Boston: Allyn and Bacon.

Slavin, R. E. (1996). Research on cooperative learning and achievement: What we know, what we need to know. *Contemporary Educational Psychology, 21,* 43–69.

Sylwester, R., & Cho, J. Y. (1992). What brain research says about paying attention. *Educational Leadership, 50*(4), 71–76.

Triandis, H. C. (1989). The self and social behavior in differing contexts. *Psychological Review, 96,* 506–520.

Vasquez, V., Muise, M. R., Adamson, S. C., & Heffernan, L. (2003). *Getting beyond "I like the book": Creating space for critical literacy in K–6 classrooms.* Newark, DE: International Reading Association.

Wiggins, G. P., & McTighe, J. (2005). *Understanding by design* (2nd ed.). Alexandria, VA: ASCD.

Zacarian, D. (1996). Learning how to teach and design curriculum for the heterogeneous class: An ethnographic study of a task-based cooperative learning group of native English and English as a second language speakers in a graduate education course. *Dissertation Abstract International.* (UMI no. 963 9055)

Zacarian, D. (2006a, March). Seriously, how did you arrive at the answer? *Essential Teacher, 3*(1), 10–11.

Zacarian, D. (2006b, December). Emergency 911. *Essential Teacher, 3*(4), 10–11.

Zacarian, D. (2007a, March). Family remedies are just the cure. *Essential Teacher, 3*(5), 10–11.

Zacarian, D. (2007b, June). The break-up. *Essential Teacher, 3*(6), 10–11.

Zacarian, D. (2007c, December). I can't go to college! *Essential Teacher, 3*(7), 10–11.

INDEX

The letter *f* following a page number denotes a figure; page numbers in italics indicate definitions.

ABOUT THE AUTHORS

Judie Haynes is the author of *Getting Started with English Language Learners: A Guide for Educators* (ASCD, 2007). She has written 25 columns on elementary education issues for the Teachers of English to Speakers of Other Languages (TESOL) publication *Essential Teacher* and has published numerous books for English language learners over the past 15 years.

Judie has taught elementary ESL for 29 years, the last 23 of which in River Edge, New Jersey. She holds a master's in language education (French) from Fairleigh Dickenson University and certifications in elementary education, ESL, and supervision. An active member of New Jersey Teachers of English to Speakers of Other Languages and Bilingual Educators (NJTESOL/NJBE), Judie was formerly the editor of the organization's quarterly publication, *Voices*, and is currently vice president and conference chair of the group. She has also been content editor and writer for the Web site, http://www.every

thingesl.net, which she cofounded with her son, Charles, in September 1999.

Judie served as chair of the Elementary Interest Section of international TESOL from 2000 to 2003 and is currently chair of the Literacy Committee. She was elected to the TESOL Nominating Committee in 2007. In addition, she served on the National Board for Professional Teaching Standards Committee from 1994 to 1998.

Judie presents professional development programs and workshops throughout the United States. She has presented at TESOL and at NJTESOL/NJBE every year for the past 17 years. She is the recipient of the New Jersey Governor's Teacher Grant (1989) and TESOL's Newberry Award for Excellence in Teaching (1993). She was also chosen as the New Jersey ESL Teacher of the Year in 1992 and the Cherry Hill School Teacher of the Year in 2006.

Debbie Zacarian is an award-winning educator, the founding director of the Center for English Language Education, and the founding and current director of the Center for Advancing Student Achievement at the Hampshire Educational Collaborative in Northampton, Massachusetts. The two centers provide professional development, licensure programming, and consulting services for educators of culturally and linguistically diverse populations. Debbie has been a columnist for TESOL's *Essential Teacher* publication since 2003 and has written 25 columns on secondary school issues. She holds a doctorate in educational policy and research from the University of Massachusetts. As a clinical faculty lecturer at the University of Massachusetts at Amherst for over a decade, she taught courses in the theories of language acquisition, language policy, assessment and evaluation, research on language acquisition, curriculum development for language and content learning, and educational administration. Debbie was also the director of the Amherst Public Schools' English Language Learners Program for over 20 years—a program that has been noted as a state and national model.

Debbie has been an educational consultant at the local, state, and national levels in English language education, closing the achievement gap, special education as it relates to students from diverse populations, and educational leadership. Recognized as a leading authority, Debbie served as an ESL certification reviewer and member of the Commissioner's Bilingual Advisory Committee for the Massachusetts Department of Education. She has delivered many papers and research presentations at the national level, including at the American Educational Research Association and TESOL.

In 1991, Debbie was cited by the Massachusetts Department of Education for her work in multicultural education, and in 1994 she was named Administrator of the Year by the Massachusetts Association of Bilingual Educators. She currently serves on the board of the Massachusetts Association of Teachers to Speakers of Other Languages.

Related ASCD Resources: English Language Learners

At the time of publication, the following ASCD resources were available (ASCD stock numbers appear in parentheses). For up-to-date information about ASCD resources, go to www.ascd.org.

Networks
Visit the ASCD Web site (www.ascd.org) and search for "networks" for information about professional edu cators who have formed groups around topics like "Language, Literacy, and Literature." Look in the "Network Directory" for current facilitators' addresses and phone numbers.

Online Courses
English Language Learners in the Mainstream (#PD09OC37)

Print Products
Classroom Instruction That Works with English Language Learners by Kathleen Flynn and Jane Hill (#106009)

Getting Started with English Language Learners: How Educators Can Meet the Challenge by Judie Haynes (#106048)

Meeting the Needs of Second Language Learners: An Educator's Guide by Judith Lessow-Hurley (#102043)

The Language-Rich Classroom: A Research-Based Framework for Teaching English Language Learners by Persida Himmele and William Himmele (#108037)

Videos and DVDs
Maximizing Learning for English Language Learners (three 35-minute videotapes with facilitator's guide) (#403326)

Raising the Literacy Achievement of English Language Learners (one DVD with facilitator's guide) (#606122)

A Visit to a Classroom of English Language Learners (one 45-minute videotape with viewer's guide) (#404447)

THE WHOLE CHILD The Whole Child Initiative helps schools and communities create learning environments that allow students to be healthy, safe, engaged, supported, and challenged. To learn more about other books and resources that relate to the whole child, visit www.wholechild education.org.

For more information: send e-mail to member@ascd.org; call 1-800-933-2723 or 703-578-9600, press 2; send a fax to 703-575-5400; or write to Information Services, ASCD, 1703 N. Beauregard St., Alexandria, VA 22311-1714 USA.